Evan,

Thanks for the support!
Hope this book can help
your mindset. Feel free to
reach out to me if
need be. Your best hasn't
come <u>YET!</u>

THE POWER OF

MICHAEL O. BENJAMIN

The Power of Yet

First paperback edition, June 2019

Book Cover Design by Vlad Nicolaescu

ISBN 978-1-0979229-6-3 (Paperback)

Published by GoldenOne Dream LLC

www.michaelobenjamin.com

For you,

my fellow visually impaired brothers and sisters.

And you,

who possesses normal visual acuity yet still placed trust in my vision.

AUTHOR'S NOTE

I wrote *The Power of Yet* primarily for the millennial that needs assistance paying off their student loans at a faster rate than they could accomplish on their own. Sometimes we just need a reminder. I paid off my $30,000+ student loans in one year after graduating college and I have the knowledge and wisdom I wish to provide for those on this pursuit.

This book is a tool that provides the necessary knowledge base to accomplish this effectively, all for an affordable price. Whether you spent money to participate in this experience or not, you've invested in yourself because at the least you're using your time to read this manuscript and I want to say: thank you.

The value provided in this book is unmatchable because you've chosen to take control of your life by making a small investment for a reward that can potentially save you thousands of dollars and time spent on paying debt. Making an investment towards a possible return on your initial investment takes risk so I applaud you.

In the simplest terms, this book provides a necessary mindset shift by allowing readers to take control of their relationship with money told through an entertaining, yet fictional tale.

Besides that, this book is also predicated off of my motivational speaking career and applied experience speaking on growth mindset. It contains information universally applicable towards any pursuit so if you're one of the lucky ones that already has financial freedom or you haven't accumulated debt yet, don't fret; this book is for you too!

I say, "If you're misguided and undecided, knowledge and wisdom can be provided!" This quote is an important theme throughout this experience because as humans we're often misguided and undecided on topics. Given that, we forget to capitalize off of the fact that someone in the universe has already experienced the issue we're trying to overcome. However, sometimes we don't forget and our ego is taking control of us as we don't want to appear like we lack information. *The Power of Yet* is the remedy for all these idiosyncrasies.

The Power of Yet experience is divided into three distinct experiences that require mastery for effectiveness. Some of these experiences as it pertains to your life may need more polishing than others. You'll encounter an experience created especially for those that have failed to maintain their faith under adversarial conditions. You'll encounter another experience created especially for those that have failed to exercise control over their thoughts. You'll encounter an additional experience created especially for those that have failed to take action when necessary.

My request is that you treat this book as your morning coffee. I personally don't drink coffee and if you're like me, treat this book as your morning drink. Read it once and return to re-read it for mastery. Let it assist you with being rewired and motivated once more to accomplish your endeavors. Sometimes we just need a reminder.

In order to receive the most value from this book, I encourage you to participate in each and every exercise following each unique experience. One experience may apply to you more than the other, but digest and master each and every experience for the sake of being equipped with the ideal mindset towards your effective growth. Sometimes we just need a reminder.

As you read this book, I challenge you to read with an open mind. Everything builds up and happens for a reason. Don't rush the process, but trust the process. I hope you have a lot of fun reading it because I had a lot of fun creating it.

Enjoy *The Power of Yet*!

—M.O.B., 2019

TABLE OF
CONTENTS

To the misguided and undecided soul

Whose trials and tribulations contribute to a loss of faith,

This phase is especially for you

As I pray peace and blessings grace your plate.

PART I

SPIRITUAL PHASE

1

I CAN'T

In the beginning, her heart was pounding aggressively, and it was about to be her turn to go up and speak. She felt she had a chip on her shoulder as she carried the burden of her struggle with public speaking, the weight of many blue whales weighing heavily on her feeble heart. Her name was Nia Akintewe.

From the outskirts of Houston, this seventeen-year-old Nigerian-American was in the midst of her first year at the local community college in Notsuoh, Texas. Nia's relatives unfamiliar with Notsuoh assumed she lived in Houston and she would often correct them, regrettably informing them she lived hours away in the notoriously boring city.

Notsuoh was a deserted wasteland. Nia grew up in a city where there wasn't much to do, and there were only two choices for inhabitants: focus or fail. Inhabitants either got influenced by boredom and participated in the negative influences that were abundantly offered, or focused and maximized the opportunity to excel under boring conditions to potentially relocate after a successful pursuit.

Boredom was an infectious disease, ruining the lives of Notsuoh residents, one life at a time. Nia fell victim to boredom's unapologetic grasp upon getting in a relationship with her abusive ex-boyfriend, Kosey. Getting in a relationship with him to fill the void of loneliness and depression she felt prior to entering college, it was easily her most regrettable decision. She had declined him a number of times, but finally accepted when she thought he was genuinely caring for her in her time of need.

Kosey, lanky and gaunt in appearance, dealt with his own insecurities, evidenced in his verbal and physical treatment towards Nia. He appeared malnourished and was the same height as her, which made him throw many verbal and physical blows her way, because he lacked self-love. Nia often wore clothing that concealed the wounds sustained. Not only that, he maintained the view he was superior to her, because his skin tone was lighter than hers. His mother was African-American, and his father was European, so he felt superior to inform her he was "mixed" and had "good hair" while referring to her as an African booty scratcher.

He constantly alerted her she couldn't accomplish her goals and would never become a woman in technology like she desired to be, for the simple fact he was misguided and undecided on his own journey. Two partners that didn't love one another, but more importantly maintained no degree of self-love resulted in an imminent catastrophe as he broke up with Nia prior to their high school graduation upon finding another girl to terrorize and they never heard from one another again.

Conveniently escaping out of the abusive relationship she lacked the courage to leave, Nia was no longer receptive to male attention as she began her collegiate career. She was closed off in her attempt to protect the last piece of her heart. Their unnecessarily long, unhealthy relationship was a result of Nia's negative fixed mindset towards men. She was nearly at her breaking point, still figuring out her own dynamic, but she knew she needed to figure it out on her own.

Although she lived many miles away from Houston, the notorious Texas heat did not discriminate. The disrespectful heat penetrated her pores without consent and would often form new blemishes at a moment's notice on her already oily skin; this produced acne that protruded out her face's surface like a pregnant woman's belly, days before her due date. They told her oily skin would guarantee she avoided wrinkles in the future though. So there was that.

Nia was noticeably short with mahogany skin full of melanin, exuding off the aroma of Cocoa Butter delicately placed on her body. Despite what seemed like admirable features on the surface, she was teased for the size of her nose, the fact she had a lower pink lip and an accompanying brown upper one, and her height, or lack thereof. These features were desired, but not when someone that looked like her possessed them. Her college classmates often claimed her nose was excessively large, her lips appeared swollen up, and she was too short to be seventeen. They also teased her about the gap between her two front teeth, so she was intentional about keeping her mouth shut when she wanted to smile. Very insecure, she would often look down as she spoke to anyone in hope that they wouldn't notice her features in her attempt to avoid any slander projected towards her.

Nia wore thick rectangular black eyeglasses over the big, brown beads of potential that were her eyes. The glasses, nearly encapsulating her entire face made it an easy avenue for her to remain the butt end of jokes. Whether she was called Steve Urkel's long lost cousin or four eyes, she wasn't a fan of any of it. She dreaded being labeled as a nerd, resulting in the concealment of her keen interest in technology as an aspiring Computer Science major, which she held behind closed doors, partly due to Kosey's reaction.

Still yet to have claimed her major, she didn't want to ignite further judgment on her character if she pursued a major in a field where the only other person that looked like her remained in the reflection she observed on her laptop screen before it turned on. Black girls were a marginalized group in technology or Computer Science fields, so why bother right?

Her colleagues condemned her for her natural hair, deeming it unprofessional in their eyes, as she looked forward to deviating from the natural look to impress others that had no regard for her well-being. These criticisms thrown at her were both vindictive and personalized.

On the verge of being underweight, Nia wore layers of clothes in her attempt to evade the slander of being classified as malnourished. She sported a couple layers of plain t-shirts under her oversized yellow hoodie to appear heftier. She wore all white Nike Air Max shoes, contrasting her black jeans. She was insecure with her height so she specifically wore these to give her an extra inch. Observing her jeans revealed skinny legs that exposed her body type. The fact that the slim boys in her class didn't get equally teased for being just as slim or slimmer than her was beyond her. The fact that they made fun of her made her chuckle as she was reminded of the Spiderman meme with the two Spidermen pointing at one another. Such were the natural struggles of a young black girl.

However, Nia's insecurities weren't limited to her appearance. She struggled immensely with public speaking. It made her stomach upset. The thought of all eyes being on her tossed her into the dark depths of despair.

Nia's fear of public speaking was deeper than meets the eye. She had an elder brother, Simba Akintewe, she looked up to as a role model, but his life was cut short, sparked by an altercation he had with law enforcement a few years prior. She witnessed the exchange and was told to recount the events leading up to the demise of her brother.

Taken into a cold, dimly lit room, the brightest light shone on her as authorities requested her to recount the event. She was in the spotlight and all eyes were on her. As the attention was placed on her, she was at a loss of words and knew what she wanted to say, but couldn't send the signal to her brain to formulate the correct words to leave her mouth due to suffered trauma from the tragedy.

During Simba's funeral, she was called up to give a public speech, and because she still suffered from immense trauma from his death, she blacked out and didn't recall the events that transpired after all eyes were on her initially. This became a recurring event when she was presented with the opportunity to speak in a public setting as she placed an emotional tie from Simba's demise with speaking. She progressed through her life, unconsciously living with a fixed mindset that she would perpetually have a negative relationship with public speaking. Not only that, the death of her brother influenced her biggest regret of getting in a relationship with her ex-boyfriend.

The fact Simba died as a result of getting away from a focused path on one occasion ran chills throughout her body when she recollected the scenario. In their boring town, people unconsciously focused or failed.

Simba was deemed a genius. He was about to be on his way to college on either a full ride Track and Field scholarship or an academic scholarship at UCLA. He always focused and excelled, earning exceptional grades and staying out of harm's way. The one time he chose to veer off on a different path was enough to end it all. His colleagues he claimed were his closest friends were suffering from underlying jealousy and set him up for failure, which was the beginning of his untimely death.

Week after week, his "friends" often went out on the weekends or wasted their time doing mundane activities, because they were bored and misguided. They invited Simba to join them, but time after time, he declined their offer. As time progressed, they grew jealous of Simba when he sporadically stated good things were happening in his life, because they saw a lack in theirs. The fact Simba nonchalantly stated his good news raised their blood pressures to dangerous levels because they thought he assumed everything came easy to him. Simba was simply humble. On one particular boring weekend where Simba agreed to go out for a movie one evening, they devised a ploy to get Simba arrested to add entertainment value to their mundane activities.

"Yo! I've got a great idea!" Connor stated with excitement.

"What?" Zane inquired with keen interest.

"We're going to the movies with Simba finally, right? Let's get him arrested."

"Whoa! You're serious? What do you mean?"

"Like as a prank or joke. We'll tell him to bring Nia to the movies and the rest is easy. Let's just get him arrested, then we'll pull up on the officer and maybe tell him it's a joke and he should be good. I think it'll be funny!"

"Say less! What are you thinking of doing?"

They initially thought the extent of the repercussions behind their actions would be a quick arrest and they would free him afterward, but deep down they didn't mind if he got arrested and his dreams and aspirations were crushed to shambles. Jealousy mixed with boredom was one dangerous mixture.

Nia remembered that day three years ago when Simba confusedly brought her to the movie theatres with him following an argument with Kosey. She was fourteen and he was seventeen. He thought he was much cooler than her and had authority over her because he had just started driving at the time. She would never forget the look of confusion he wore as he wondered why his "friends" operated the way they did.

"Ni Ni! Hurry up! Get out my car already," Simba stated.

"That's not even your car Simba," Nia began. "You know Dad got you that car anyway! But don't rush me!"

"Where are they at man? I don't know why they told me to bring you here, but the homies told me to bring you here with me."

"Maybe they want you to be nice to me because you're always so mean!"

"Aye man, shut up! You should have had little Kosey bring you here then."

"He's stupid! But don't talk about him like that."

"You're hilarious. But I just realized something. It's funny how people that don't know you personally are more willing to support you than people you've known forever that you call your friends."

"You shut up! Why do you say that though?"

"I'm just thinking how these two are supposed to be my friends, but they didn't even really congratulate me on UCLA or even any of my accomplishments in the past. It was always random people supporting me. It's almost like they feel threatened by me or something."

"Simba, I think you're thinking about it too deeply."

"Eh, you might be right Ni Ni. Well, let's go."

Still perplexed and alarmed at the fact his "friends" didn't show up when they invited him and pestered him to bring Nia along, Simba and Nia watched the movie, both fixed on their phones for a majority of the movie. They didn't even recall the title of the movie. The only thing they recalled was the inflection of the speakers nearly shattering their eardrums to smithereens. Nia sporadically glanced over at Simba during the screening and witnessed his phone screen shining on his mahogany skin, as he texted aggressively wondering where his "friends" were. As the movie ended, Nia and Simba began to leave as Simba looked frustrated.

"Did you get in contact with your friends?" Nia inquired.

"No! I'm going to scold them for that when I see them. That's disrespectful."

"Yeah. How did you feel about the movie though?"

"Man, I don't know what movie you were watching, but I can barely even hear your question. Those speakers were way too loud and my ears are still ringing right now."

"Yeah. Mine are kind of the same. I think I heard you?"

"I'm never going out ever again! I'm just going to focus from here on out and get ready to go to UCLA in the Fall. There's too much nonsense going on in Notsuoh and I'm not trying to be a bum and fail like the rest of them."

This was the last interactive conversation Nia had with Simba before their dynamic changed forever.

As they stepped outside, police cars swayed in their direction. Initially, they didn't make anything of it until a couple officers approached Simba rapidly and yelled out a few obscenities before telling him to get down. Neither Nia nor Simba heard what was stated.

"What?" Simba inquired with his hands spread out confusedly nearly as far as if he was on a cross being crucified.

"Are you threatening us with that tone? Stop being aggressive!"

"Wait!" Simba stated animatedly, flailing his arms as he went into panic mode. "I just saw a movie and I can't hear what—"

One shot to his right forearm was the beginning of the end. An officer in the distance assumed he wasn't complying as the other officers nearby chastised him for pulling his trigger. Simba's "friends" revealed themselves, crying excessively as they informed the officers that they falsely reported a murder, describing Simba and stating he kidnapped a girl they described as Nia. They were arrested for defamation of character shortly after.

As Simba recovered in the hospital, Nia realized he wasn't the same prior to his nearly fatal encounter. He seemed more extreme with his emotions, either extremely happy or extremely depressive. Other times he would be nonchalant about everything. He eventually made a full recovery physically, but never made a full recovery spiritually or mentally as he lost the charming faith he once possessed. Losing his UCLA scholarship opportunities, Nia avoided the conversation and wondered how it occurred.

There was one particular day where Simba gave away a plethora of his stuff to Nia. He was known to be a giver, but this day was different. One thing after the other, he gave it to her.

"Nia!" Simba yelled from his room in their old house. "I know I'm giving you all this stuff, but remember, if you're misguided and undecided, knowledge and wisdom can be provided!"

"What does that even mean?" Nia inquired confused.

"Exactly what I said! It's grown man talk between me and Dad. If you know it, then you know it! I'm busy though and working on something, so I'll see you later!" Simba replied energetically.

This was the last interactive conversation Nia had with Simba.

Simba was having one of his extremely happy moods and Nia didn't know what to make of it at the time. Hours later, Nia was informed he committed suicide. His struggles were detailed in a written letter. He claimed the altercation with law enforcement changed his life for the worst where he fell into a depressive state partly due to the altercation, but more so because he felt betrayed by individuals he claimed to be his brethren. The tipping point was the high medical bills sitting at astronomical levels. Money became an issue to him and took control of his life, and when he lost his UCLA scholarship, in his eyes he lost it all. Simba's "friends" plotted to get him arrested, but their prank went too far, resulting in an eventual self-inflicted blow.

If Nia learned one thing from Simba's death besides her desire to go to UCLA to live the life he deserved, it was that one time is more than enough to lose it all. The bad outweighs the good. However, her brother's legacy was forever remembered, so he was perpetually alive, gone only in the physical form. Ever since that day, she made a promise with herself to never allow money issues to stress her to the point of taking her own life. Culturally, money was a stressor for many, but it was important to be intentional about one's relationship with money, and taking control of it, rather than letting it take control of you, and your mind. Nia's father reminded her of that frequently following Simba's death as he often coached her on tips and strategies to pay off the student loans she would accrue in an accelerated fashion.

Regardless of whether or not Nia thought about her brother, she was now scarred in her ability to perform public speaking. Her public speaking was as good as it was going to get and she would always faint no matter the situation. She was fixed in this mindset and very sure of it.

Her name was called by her professor. A hefty woman with a mole on her right cheek and pale wrinkly skin, most of the students couldn't tell whether she was smiling or if her face was just wrinkled, but she was genuinely smiling at Nia.

"Nia! You're up!"

They were nearly halfway through the semester and this was their first project where they had to perform public speaking. The rest of the class was most likely about to find out Nia's little secret.

Palms sweating and beads of sweat forming on the surface of her forehead, she made her way up to the front of the classroom and turned around to face her peers. Her professor welcomed her with a genuine, yellow crooked smile and encouraged her to begin, nodding her head profusely in the process.

"Go ahead, sweetie." She displayed an animated hand gesture. "Begin."

Nia glanced over at her and then looked back at her colleagues. Various confusing faces spanned the room of about 20 individuals anticipating her speech. Half of these initially confused figures grew into menacing smiles. They now looked like monsters preparing to attack her as she grew defensive while being confronted by her perpetrators.

The room was spinning and Nia wasn't certain what to do. She was having an out of body experience and felt like she was from the outside looking in, attempting to return back into her body to perform simple bodily functions. Fingers twitching, it felt like an eternity had commenced as she attempted to take control of herself.

Nia began pondering deeply about her brother's letter regarding his financial struggles his mind couldn't control. She remembered being questioned by the authorities with the bright light shining on her in that cold, isolated room that lacked forgiveness. She started to feel cold again, despite having layers of clothes underneath her signature yellow hooded sweatshirt.

She was able to slightly focus and zero in on her classmates once more. She wasn't aware of how much time had elapsed. Now they all transformed into blurry silhouettes as her glasses grew foggy.

She blacked out.

"Nia!"

She faintly heard her name called, whilst hearing a familiar ringing noise when she was about to faint from attempting to speak.

It was all black.

"Nia! Wake up Nia!"

Nothingness.

Nia woke up abruptly. She quickly realized she passed out in her classroom before giving her speech. She also realized her entire class knew about what happened to her. How embarrassing. How would she go back to any of her classes ever again? That was a topic for another day.

Although Nia was now aware she had fainted, she was still confused as she hovered her fingers over her face in an attempt to fix her glasses. To her surprise, they were nowhere to be found on her face. Her eyes meandered her surroundings aimlessly, and the first thing she noticed with her limited vision was a meme pasted on the wall many feet away from her. She could see enough to only see a blurry silhouette but knew it was a meme. Not only that, her ears ceased ringing and worked perfectly as she heard Beyoncé's music ringing throughout the premises of her surroundings.

"I like my negro nose with Jackson Five nostrils."

Nia felt chills running through her body as she recollected the number of times she was teased for her nose. Hearing those lyrics spewed upon her waking up empowered her like no other force or IV could. Regardless, every time she heard Beyoncé's "Formation," she was proud to be from Texas, even if it wasn't Houston. She was practically a Houston resident, and no one could tell her she lived on the outskirts when Beyoncé became a topic of conversation. Because Nia's town was a boring one, everyone seemed to grapple onto Houston culture for the sake of not being excluded from Houston pride. The music selection she heard threw her off, but a couple more scans of her surroundings and Nia was aware she was in the school's infirmary.

It was filled with various attractive gadgets she hadn't laid her eyes on since her last annual physical examination, so it struck her with a bout of amazement. The things doctors utilized and understood never ceased to amaze her. The aroma of the room she was placed in had a homely atmosphere with fluorescent bulbs shining brightly on her.

It was then, she began to panic to a small degree, but she made her best effort not to imagine that the spotlight was on her. After all, she didn't want to pass out again. She began perspiring slightly while attempting to deviate her mind from the fact the lighting in the room made her feel like she had to speak again. Attempting to avoid a relapse, her handicap eyes wandered around the room with a sense of urgency, despite the fact she felt like her eyeballs were about to explode out of each of their sockets at a moment's notice.

She attempted to focus her gaze on the meme once more in an attempt to view it clearer for reassurance it was what she initially thought it was. She suffered from nearsightedness. This meant objects close to her were clear, but objects in the distance were blurry. Many of her classmates gifted with exceptional vision didn't understand this concept until she explained it to them. Beyoncé kept infiltrating her ears as she squinted her eyes trying to make out what the meme was, but she failed to.

"Okay ladies, now let's get in formation!"

"Because I slay!"

A random voice was heard yelling in the nearby distance, startling Nia.

"Sorry! Didn't mean to scare you there."

It was the nurse. She was a young-looking stylish woman that couldn't have been pushing past thirty years old. The nurse possessed a unique swagger to her walk and the way she communicated that made Nia feel comfortable instantly. Her dark complexion was enough to welcome her. She wore a neon green wig, sported scrubs, and wore various rings on her fingers and different colored bracelets, giving herself a unique appearance.

"I hope you're alright now sweetie," she began. Nia squinted to look at her, scrunching her nose in her attempt to see the nurse clearly. The nurse walked closer and Nia was welcomed with a whiff of her aroma, a fresh alternative to the smell of the room. "What's that?"

"I can't..." Nia replied maintaining a throbbing headache.

The nurse quickly realized something appeared different about Nia.

"Oh! Your glasses. Wait just one second! I got you."

She quickly left the room once more and returned with Nia's thick black spectacles in a jiffy.

Nia never thought the day would come, but she was pretty excited to be reunited with her glasses she deeply resented. The same nemesis she had a sworn issue with that contributed to some of the slanders she had to endure on a daily basis was back in her possession. It was a love/hate relationship they shared. The fact that they would fog up when she was nervous or in a humid area like her city, made her disgusted. This occurred more often than not. The fact that they would be a liability to function when it was raining heavily outside, made her disgusted. However, they were a necessary ugly accessory for her to view the beautiful world. She lay them back on her eyes. She felt refreshed.

"Well Nia," the nurse began. She analyzed a tool that was plugged to Nia's arm and pressed buttons, making a tapping noise because of her long, polished white nails, sharp enough to penetrate the bone of a living human. Nia found them fascinating since she personally didn't typically keep up with her appearance. She kept makeup in her bag, but never used it. "I hope you're feeling better. Your vital signs are good, but you'll want to get some rest when you leave and sip on some fluids. Water is preferred, but Gatorade would work too. You want to get some good electrolytes in your body girl!"

Nia simply stared at the nurse as she presented herself animatedly with enthusiasm. She stopped her enthusiasm, seemingly absorbing Nia's diminished energy and reciprocating her gaze.

"Uh Nia, you're making things awkward. But anyway, basically you passed out in your class when you were about to give a speech. Like I said, you're good now, but we think you may have just been dehydrated at the time and the stress of that situation contributed to your fainting. Have you ever had anything like that happen before when you had to give a speech?"

Nia's pupils widened; her heart was pacing like a lion hunting a gazelle as it attempted to escape where it beat. She initiated her best attempt at making her lips move, twitching them slightly.

"I...can't," she muttered narrowly.

The nurse placed a finger on her own chin, appearing to be in deep thought, captivated by Nia's couple words, separated by a dramatic silence. She knew Nia wasn't a huge communicator thus far, so she placed a high value on anything Nia said.

"You can't what?"

"I can't."

Nia stared off into the distance, evading a gaze with the nurse as she grew cognizant of her insecurities.

The nurse quickly realized that this wasn't a typical situation of a student being dehydrated and passing out.

"Okay honey. Wait a minute."

She walked a couple of feet to retrieve a pen and began scribbling words on a sticky note. Nia assumed she would be handed this sticky note.

The nurse finished her manuscript.

"Nia, your father is here to pick you up if you haven't picked up on the fact our session is over, *so* you're free to go into the lobby and go home."

Nia glanced at her with a confused gaze as if the nurse had just directed disrespectful bants her way. The nurse crossed her arms and looked back at Nia. Nia didn't fret, despite this slight change in the nurse's attitude.

"I can't."

The nurse retaliated, finally losing her patience, but still maintaining a level of professionalism.

"Nia sweetie! Listen to me."

She moved closer to Nia and put her arm around her. "Between you and me, I know whatever you went through, it was daunting, and I'm coming to you woman to woman," she continued as she looked left and right as if she was searching for a fly on the wall nearby. "I'm coming to you black woman to black woman, if you need some help, *please* have your father give me a call, but we have more patients coming in so you *have* to leave right now."

The nurse let out a reluctant sigh as she stood up and showed Nia out the door. She noticed the nurse had the formation of poignant tears appearing to fall down her face momentarily. She sincerely cared about Nia, but she was caught in a dilemma where she had to perform her job; this was a battle many faced daily, making money for the owner of their institution while receiving a fraction of return for their contribution. Nia understood, making it easier to walk into the lobby and be in the midst of the real world once again. She wanted to continue hiding in the secluded room, but quite frankly, that wasn't a feasible option.

As soon as she arrived in the lobby, she saw her father, Rufus Akintewe. The moment their eyes met, he rushed towards her and welcomed her with a warm embrace. She needed that. It was a long, short day for her.

Letting go, Mr. Akintewe followed the front desk's directions as he signed out. The nurse rushed over to her father and whispered something in his ear Nia couldn't make out. She figured it had to be related to the sticky note she scribbled on, because she handed it to him afterwards, and her father gave an acknowledged nod of approval. Nia was left befuddled, to say the least.

The nurse retrieved back to her sanctuary Nia so desired to return to. Nia and her father walked side by side leaving the premises of the school ground, an unnecessary battlefield to dwell on any longer from Nia's perspective.

As they arrived outside and the door to the office shut, Nia's father glanced back for confirmation, before beginning to start a conversation that was meant for the two of them.

"You want to talk about it? What happened today, sweetie?"

Nia felt comfort in hearing her father's deep voice, a symbol of protection. If he told her everything was going to be alright, it was going to be alright in her eyes. Despite the feeling of comfort from his words, Nia's feelings of inadequacy outweighed her desire to openly seek comfort with her father. She scrunched her face as she attempted to keep up with his steady pace since he had an unfair advantage on her of long legs Nia wished she would have in the future in hope she wasn't done growing taller.

"I can't."

"You can't what?"

Nia evaded eye contact with her father as she let out the embarrassing circumstance.

"I fainted from trying to do my speech presentation in class today."

Her father laughed. She immediately regretted coming out of her shell and telling him. "Don't be so hard on yourself sweetie." He maintained a steady laugh as he used his left index finger to push his glasses upward to sit back in place on his face. "The same actually happened to me one time when I had to give a speech for my class *way* back in the day."

Nia confusedly analyzed him, waiting for him to admit he was lying to her, but he didn't budge. This was news to her. She slightly felt better, but still regretted informing him to a certain degree.

He looked up as he glanced off into the distance. "Yup, I remember that day. Just waking up and not knowing where I was." He lay a finger on his chin, implanting a finger in the scruffy bush protruding out while unlocking the door and opening her door for her. "You really are my daughter."

Despite the similarity in their situations, Nia's father didn't know the source of her panic. He didn't know about her abusive relationship with Kosey. He didn't know her public speaking trauma was partly traced to Simba's death. Although Nia was his daughter, Simba was of no relation to him, because he was Nia's half-brother from her mother's past relationship. Her father welcomed him like he was his own child, but wasn't as impacted on his death as Nia was. Nia grew closer to Simba because they spent incalculable quality time together and competing with one another. Nia's mother's impact was another story for both Nia and her father.

Nia never met her mother, as she only heard from Simba and her father that she passed away from giving birth to her. Simba was barely old enough to know his mother, but he swore he knew her to acquire a competitive edge over Nia. Not only did Nia never meet her, the extent to which she knew her mother was the fact her mother crowned her her name as she took her last breath before passing. Her last words were instructing Nia's father to give Nia her name, meaning purpose in Swahili. Her father's interpretation of the event was that her mother knew she was passing away as a sacrifice, and Nia was created with that purpose in mind. She was to be the golden child and perpetuate their legacy. Her father told her that her mother lived in all their spirits and she was specifically Nia's guardian angel. Nia often watched videos of her, witnessing her smooth skin full of melanin attached to the soft, unique inflection of her voice.

Nia's father often had random bouts of guilt as he recalled her death. He had survivor's guilt because he was a survivor and watched his wife take her last breath. He emotionally blamed the medical field, but more specifically blamed the nurses at the time when he gathered his thoughts for a more reasonable judgment. As Nia's mother gave birth to Nia, he picked up on the fact she appeared unusual as he ran to scramble and alert the nurses, but they simply told him Nia's mother was not a priority. A couple of minutes later, and she was gone.

Her father often preached about the fact that there was a deep prevalence of racism and discrimination in the medical field towards black women when it came to handling them with care. He would often communicate this to Nia with passion, citing examples with data showing the statistics backing up his claims. Nia didn't make much of it and let him rant, because that was his reality. When he referenced her mother, this was enough to capture Nia's attention and inform her of the fact that it was an issue. She recognized it was an issue initially, but when her mother was brought into the picture, it shed a different light on the situation.

As the car maneuvered toward their house, Nia sat in silence, coming to terms with her inability to avoid fainting when giving a speech. Her father picked up on the silence and turned the radio on, because he didn't want to harass her with a conversation. The first sound she heard shifted her entire mood as she danced along.

It was Megan Thee Stallion's song, "Big Ole Freak."

Nia's father shook his head as he witnessed his daughter dancing and smiling effortlessly. She was in her element and he was happy about that.

"What are these kids listening to these days?"

"It's Megan Thee Stallion Dad! This is one of her old songs!"

Nia continued dancing to the beat and repeating the lyrics, not missing a beat and failing to censor the curse words.

"Hey! Don't cuss in front of me. That's disrespectful," he corrected her playfully. "This is a great beat, I'm not going to lie. And I can tell she can actually rap. She needs to rap on more classic beats though to put it to the test."

Nia smiled like she had prepared the most potent response to refute her father's point. "She actually went to a lot of radio shows and showed her ability to rap in the beginning of her career." She smirked as her father's facial expression changed to being shocked, as he gave a congratulatory nod.

"Oh wow, okay I have respect for her game. Not a lot of rappers are doing that these days so much respect to her. I'm a fan then."

"Yup. Told you!"

"Hey, relax with that excessive energy."

"Alright old man," she began, anticipating her father's response in her attempt to elicit a reaction out of him. He smiled and shook his head. Mission accomplished. She stretched her little arms in the car as she yawned and was noticeably in a better mood. "Well, it's the weekend now so that's good."

Her father saw this as an opportunity to check in with her since she was now in a better mental state. He turned off the radio.

"Well...how was your day sweetie? Aside from all that stuff that happened?"

"I guess it was good up until I got embarrassed."

"You guess, or it was good? Which one?"

She rolled her eyes.

"It was good, Dad." Her father was a motivational speaker and often would dive deep into human behavior and analyze specific word usage. "I just can't though."

He appeared slightly annoyed.

"I've been asking you. You can't what?"

"I can't. I can't do anything. I can't do anything successfully. I can't be successful. I feel like a failure. I can't."

He appeared even more annoyed as if she spat in his cereal he consumed that morning.

"Now hold up! What did I tell you about speaking negativity into your life? The power of words are so powerful, you need to be careful what you wish for because negativity is not a force to be reckoned with. The power of the mouth is powerful, so prophesy your words into fruition!"

Nia puckered her lips, appearing annoyed as she listened to his spiel.

"It's time for our routine! Who are you and who am I?"

"I'm Nia Akintewe, and you're my father who loves me," she replied unenthusiastically.

"What do you deserve?"

"I deserve all the love in the world," she replied with noticeably more energy.

"What are the three pillars for financial freedom to get rid of your student loan debt or overcome anything you encounter?"

"Believe. Plan. Execute."

"Why should you practice patience?"

"Patience allows me to take risks without repercussions, because it gives me the mindset to focus on the fact that I have time."

"And why is gratitude so important?"

"You can't be great without being grateful, it's in the word if you reverse the letters."

"Good! You have to love yourself sweetie. You have to learn to love yourself before you can engage in love with someone else. With our routine, I inform you I love you, but you must love yourself first before you engage with someone else because that isn't fair to the other person if you aren't fully loving of yourself or know a great sense of direction in your life."

Nia felt a burning guilt in her spirit. As her father spoke, she thought about her regretful relationship with Kosey. It was as if her father knew about her past she desired to erase from her memory.

"Those words of affirmation are a lot more powerful than you think too. I saw you change as we progressed with the questions. You've been asking me about financial literacy for a while. We're going to touch on some financial stuff later on, but let me put you on introductory game. This is prerequisite information to the financial literacy game I'm going to lace you with. Just trust me and follow along during this journey."

"Here we go again," Nia responded as she exercised her thumb, scrolling on

Twitter searching for a funny tweet to disengage from the situation, regretting her 'I can't' rant.

Her father was not amused.

"If you don't put that phone down," he began. "Social media has crippled the mind and it even makes people think they're better than others! You want to dive into the financial information so bad, I'll just give you a quick tip: take a day off from that social media poison. It isn't real. You're running away from our conversation, but you should be running away from social media for a day! It's a poisonous invention that's used to capitalize on insecurities. It's the cousin of boredom, an obvious disease. Therefore, social media is a disease. Look around Notsuoh. Everyone's constantly on it acting a fool and plagued in the mind to the point they think it's reality. It's good when you use it for a purpose to provide value, but most people, including yourself, don't. You better tighten up and focus if you don't want to lose yourself. That's all I'm saying."

She set her phone down and gave her father her undivided attention, noticeably angrily, but understanding his point at the same time.

"Whatever Dad. You're right."

"Your health has to be a priority Nia, and it starts with up here, mentally. Take care of your mental health and care about your physical health. How many hours of sleep did you get last night by the way?"

"I don't know."

"No, just understand me," he continued as Nia began glancing out the window with her arms folded. "You have to sleep! Make sure you rest when we get home. Remember like I always tell you: less is more! When you get those extra hours of sleep you need, you'll have less operating hours in the day, but you'll be more energetic and equipped to accomplish a lot more in that smaller window versus being tired with more time and not being effective.

"Nia baby, listen. I know you're always in a rush and eager to talk about money, but you have to master preliminary steps before we get there. Most people don't understand that and assume you just wake up one day and get rid of all your debt instantly. It doesn't work that way." Her body grew less tense as she attempted to listen to what her father had to say. "Everyone has their own unique gift and *you* must find yours."

She didn't appear moved.

"Listen here, baby girl. I got something really special for you right here! This is about to be a golden gem I shouldn't even give out for free!"

She rolled her eyes once more because she knew it was her father acting excessively dramatic as a motivational speaker. She didn't think she needed his motivation. After all, she was an adult in college. What did her father know about life?

"You know," her father continued his speech. "If I was at a speaking engagement right now, I would tell the audience to write down everything I'm saying right now and they would write it down and if they didn't understand it that day, eventually they would understand it. I know you view me as your old man that doesn't know anything, but I've seen and experienced things you haven't and you can gain value from me. I'm still learning this fatherhood stuff, but we'll learn together as we continue along the way."

Nia was taken aback.

"It's like he's reading my mind," she thought.

She still maintained her stance of doubting herself.

"I can't," she muttered to herself quietly.

"What did you say?"

"Oh, nothing!"

"Okay sweetie, let me continue. Before you identify your strength, you have to take control of your spirituality; this is having a belief system. When it comes to anything in life, you have to believe the idea before taking action to ensure it comes into fruition. You have to believe the idea before it goes into planning. Belief. Believe! You have to believe that you will get over your fear of public speaking. Believe, then you plan, and then you execute. This is why we perform our daily regimen when I take you to school. We're going to talk about this more later, but I first want to give you time to rest. I just wanted to give you a high level explanation of this."

"I can't Dad. Everyone was making fun of me in my class and laughing at me.

I just can't. I don't know why you don't understand that, but I just can't. I can't."

"I understand, because I was in your shoes before. You can, and you will." He continued driving in silence for a couple moments before continuing the conversation. "When was the last time you read a book?"

She lay a finger on her chin as she scrunched her nose attempting to recall her last experience looking at words and flipping pages. It had been quite a while since she read a book, because she never performed assigned readings in her classes. Nia didn't like being told what to do, especially when it came to reading. If she was going to read, she would read with her own consent.

"I would say probably when I was reading your draft of that book you wrote that never came out," she replied with a playful banter.

"Come on! So my daughter got jokes like that? I didn't know I was in the car here with Kevin Hart!" They both laughed genuinely. "But I want to give you the opportunity to get back into reading since that was a long time ago. You said that your classmates will make fun of you for what happened to you?"

"Not just that, but they make fun of me for everything," Nia began speaking passionately, feeling her eyes watering up. "My glasses. My hair. My nose. I talk. I breathe. They make fun of me. I can't."

"I understand you," he replied genuinely. "I'm going to recommend you start with *The Four Agreements* by Don Miguel Ruiz. I think you'll find value in the second agreement. I'll give you the book when we get home."

"What's the second agreement?"

He let out a ferocious laugh. He was passionate about reading.

"You'll have to do your homework, baby girl. You've got the entire weekend and it's a short read. And you probably didn't realize it, but you do read noticeably faster than your peers and the average person, so use that and recognize that. I don't want to hear 'I can't' anymore. Rebuke it!"

Nia thought about the accuracy of her father's claim. She did find the act of reading a quick activity for her, but it didn't occur to her everyone didn't have the same experience as her. When you're gifted at something, it comes natural to you so you don't think about the fact other people have to work harder to be just as good as you when you aren't exuding as much energy or effort as they are. Nia was just realizing this phenomenon and was beginning to see why her father was being paid for speaking.

He was good. He was effortlessly good.

"Another thing to remember sweetie," he began as he yawned. "Most people in the world have a fear of public speaking and I'm going to want you to be familiar with a growth mindset. You know what a growth mindset is?"

Nia's thought process was to break down the word.

"Isn't it just a way of thinking where you know you can grow?"

To her surprise, her father was content with her response.

"Exactly! Growth mindset is basically the mentality or mindset where you know that your basic talent isn't limited to where it's at and it can be developed over time."

"That's basically what I said, but you said it differently."

"More or less what you said, sweetie. So with a growth mindset, it's important that we distinguish between its opposite. What do you think the opposite of a growth mindset is?"

"A non-growth mindset?"

He laughed.

"You are *so* cute. Another true statement, but the mindfulness term we use is fixed mindset. You're basically fixed in your way of thinking and think that your ability or talent is limited to where it's at and can't be developed. Right now, you're operating in a fixed mindset and we want to rebuke that spirit out of you!"

Nia grew offended.

"Me? Fixed mindset? How?"

"Think about your word choice. You keep repeating the phrase, 'I can't' when we're discussing your day or overcoming public speaking."

"I can't," Nia replied jokingly.

Her father didn't receive it as a joke. As they approached a red light, he grabbed her hand with his veins popping out and embracing her as he looked into her eyes intensely. He had a muscular build, so loosened his grip slightly. "You *have* to be confident in yourself, sweetie. It's a survival skill I'm going to need you to develop. I'm going around the world speaking about success and my own child isn't taking the lessons from me. That's messing up the brand. I'm going to need you to tighten up for me."

He let go of her hand and put his other hand back on the wheel.

"I'm going to help you identify your strength and say you have great discipline. You know what discipline means?"

"Discipline? Like self-discipline? Isn't it just being able to have control of yourself or something like that?"

"Yes ma'am, that's exactly what it is! Don't be afraid you'll say the wrong answer. Own your words!"

"Discipline though? I don't think that's one of my strengths if I'm being honest with you, Dad."

He used his left index finger to push up his glasses.

"We don't view our talents as talents because of the fact it comes easy to us, and we think everyone has it like that. But think about it, obesity is a huge issue, right? Discipline is about self-control and not everyone is an expert on self-discipline. Because you can simply control what you eat, that's your unique gift in my opinion."

He wore a smirk that screamed he had an ulterior motive for saying this, but Nia didn't know what that was.

They pulled into the driveway and went inside. Their home was a large secluded house, nearing the size of an impressive mansion, with African antiques arbitrarily placed all over the area. It smelled like fresh incense was being burned as they were welcomed with a whiff of it upon their arrival.

Nia's father ran to his lengthy library and scanned the selections, rummaging through the books. He pulled out a book and she noticed the style from a mile away. It was *The Four Agreements*. He placed the book in her hand, simultaneously as he maintained a grip on it.

"I know you don't have the greatest GPA, but you definitely have a talent at reading relatively fast, so I have higher expectations for you than I have for anyone else. I know you are busy with your UCLA appeal application and other stuff so I'll give you one week to read this and report back to me. Deal?"

Nia looked down at the book and her father's powerful clutch on it.

"Yes sir!"

He let go of his grip and it was now in her hands. She felt the book and stared at it in awe. Its surface had a unique finish that couldn't be described, and its aesthetically pleasing appearance made her excited to start reading books again. It had been quite some time, but she still felt a sense of confidence in her accelerated reading ability.

Nia retrieved back to her room for privacy. She needed to mentally unpack everything that had escalated throughout her day. She felt new-found confidence after the car ride home with her father. When she would start driving herself home was a topic of discussion for another day, but she was satisfied at this moment to say the least.

She had no regard for her dusty, black backpack and threw it across the room. Its rough condition suffered from years of wear and tear. Taking off her shoes welcomed her room with a sweaty aroma from her socks. She then threw herself aggressively on her bed, lying down on her back. Staring toward the ceiling fan oscillating like a perpetual rollercoaster of peace, she thought about the possibility that she might get out of her depressive approach to public speaking.

"Home sweet home."

2

FEAR

A couple days had elapsed. Nia finished *The Four Agreements* the day before, days in advance of her father's deadline. They discussed it and it made her feel slightly more confident in herself. Despite her new-found confidence she thought she now had after finishing the book and having a conversation with her father, she was slowly beginning to revert back to the old version of herself that gravitated towards a fixed mindset of taking the judgment from her peers personally. The voices of doubt in her head were creeping in. Her confidence was deteriorating.

"Don't take anything personal," she thought to herself. Although she understood it and attempted to embrace it, it was a lot to ask of her. Getting over her fear of public speaking? Forget about it. That wasn't a feasible task she could fathom in her head. She was suffering from information overload and pressure to fulfill everything she desired to accomplish. From her UCLA college appeal application to avoiding another failed written driver test, she realized all her insecurities were predicated by one thing: fear.

Nia was living in fear. Fear was a daunting emotion. It was a scary spirit. The fear of not being able to choose between focusing versus failing in her city gave her a headache. The fear of not rising above her public speaking hurdle made her want to vomit. The fear of not being able to live out her full potential made her skin crawl. The fear of paying her student loan debt for decades haunted her. The fear of assimilating to the groupthink that having student loans for an extended period of time was acceptable was daunting. It all scared her greatly.

She blinked her eyes rapidly as she witnessed the silhouette of a familiar figure. It was Simba. He walked gracefully towards her as the light revealed his angelic aura. Nia could not believe what her eyes revealed to her. Her brother that died was in the flesh in front of her. Could this really be him? Had he been hiding the entire time?

"Ni Ni," he began. He crowned her that nickname. It was really her brother she was standing in front of. From his distinct muscular build to his unique voice and curly high top bald fade hairstyle he sported, she knew this was Simba. But why was he alive? "Ni Ni. I need you to really hear me out. I'm counting on you and rooting for you. You obviously have a lot of insecurities you're dealing with. We know that. Your written driving test. Your fear of public speaking because of what happened to me."

Nia's heart raced as she grew fearful.

"How do you know about the speaking thing?"

She glanced at him and then her thoughts scattered and she realized something was slightly off.

"You've got to get it together, Ni Ni," he began. "I'm rooting for you, but if you keep living in fear and don't maximize those insecurities you've got, your future doesn't look bright and you'll forever live in fear with that fixed lifestyle. Your future self on this self-destructive path can tell you right now. Nia?"

Nia grew even more fearful. She loved her brother and cherished the conversations they often had organically prior to his death, but this interaction began to scare her. Times had changed. She recognized this wasn't a realistic occurrence, but participated in it for what it was.

"Yes brother?"

"Your future self that has a perpetual fixed mindset is counting on you to get rid of it for the benefit of both of y'all."

"My...future self?"

In the blink of an eye, Nia rose as she felt her bed soaked in sweat. She rubbed her forehead and felt her body to feel the moisture. Placing her hand where her heart lay, she felt the rhythm of an African drum failing to miss a beat.

It was all a dream.

She knew it was too good to be true as she recollected what had just transpired. This wasn't the first time she had dreamt of him, but it certainly had caught her by surprise since it had been a while since she last dreamt of him. Simba had been gone for three years, so she couldn't place a finger on why she was being revisited by him after not being visited by him for over a year. She thought she had come to terms with his passing, but it appeared to her that wasn't the case.

Nia was already aware of the fact she was living in fear. It didn't take her brother coming to her as a messenger to let her know that. She was spiritual and a believer in God, but she wasn't the most spiritually awakened individual when she needed to be. In times where she felt fear more prevalent or was placed in any minor inconvenience, she would ignore the importance of spiritual power and not place much faith in God as her savior. Her relationship with God thus far was situational to say the least. Her father raised his concerns to her about her relationship with God sporadically, but she didn't think she needed to change it. He would tell her having a fixed mindset was potentially killing her by the day.

It was the last day of her weekend off before returning to that wretched environment she called her community college. Fond of Kendrick Lamar's *Damn* album, she played track 12 as she began cleaning her room. Cleaning her room while listening to music and knowing she didn't have to attend that warzone was quite a liberating experience for her.

As Nia cleaned, she attempted to direct her mind away from her dream and her various insecurities that consistently plagued her psyche. She redirected her energy specifically to the beat of the song as it played unnecessarily loud on her speakers, absorbing the inflection of the beat as it ran through her soul. She hummed the lyrics she naturally picked up on because she played this specific song so many times. This was her idea of a spiritual experience, but it lasted for no longer than some minutes; she was hit with reality once more, like she received a knockout punch from a professional boxer. Life was undefeated, and Nia was winless.

Knockout.

Nia randomly recalled the previous week when she lost consciousness at school from attempting to speak. Recollecting that event was the catalyst for falling in an abyss of deeper thoughts. She then recalled Simba's passing and the feelings she felt while being interrogated and given the stage to recollect what happened. She then recalled being instructed to speak about Simba at his funeral. The dream came to mind next. The negative feeling extracted from her upon hearing her future wouldn't be bright as a result of the future version of herself counting on her placed an immense amount of pressure on how she proceeded. She didn't like how she felt in any of these situations and regretted being wired with her introspective characteristic.

Fear.

Nia recollected her relationship with college. She had been putting off her UCLA application for quite some time as the deadline was approaching and she had no sense of direction for how to approach her personal statement. The idea of college and being tossed into a new environment for survival made her stomach turn like a washing machine's cycle. She thought about leaving her father's residence as she grew nauseous. Being tossed in a new environment out of her element of comfortability and being expected to thrive sounded unrealistic to her. She pondered on her feelings towards the appeal application process as she stared at her computer screen for hours, making little to no progress.

Fear.

College was a foreign concept to Nia that she couldn't seem to comprehend. Although she felt ignorant about college, she felt confident enough to know her high school failed to prepare her for her collegiate experience, physically and mentally. Because college was foreign to her, she placed a high amount of weight on it, because it was an unknown realm she was stepping into. She attended her local community college, but she desired to transfer to UCLA for the sake of Simba. She had a recurring fear of not getting accepted into UCLA since she was now filing an appeal, which was the first hurdle. Another hurdle she grew aware of was if she would even survive and thrive while she was there. She was an aspiring Computer Science major and the lack of representation for students that looked like her in that field discouraged her. Her parents attended great colleges, receiving admirable degrees so pressure to perform and carry on the legacy for them contributed to her fears as well.

She turned off her music sound system and retrieved her laptop. Upon separating the top and bottom flaps and turning it on, she was presented with her application open in one tab and opened an additional tab, going to YouTube.

As she began to type into the search bar, her search suggestions popped up to her dismay:

How to get into UCLA

Day in the life of a UCLA student

UCLA college vlogs

Nia was shocked all her search history was centered on UCLA because it hadn't occurred to her she watched videos on it so frequently. As a Texas native, she was obsessed with the idea of traveling to California, growing up her entire life expressing her desire to start a life in The Golden State. As Simba died, she shifted her purpose from simply desiring to live in California to wanting to live in California through being accepted into UCLA. It was her dream school now and the only one she planned on finishing the rest of her collegiate career at. From her perspective, if she couldn't get into UCLA, she didn't need to finish college.

Nia played a recommended vlog of a student at UCLA discussing the life of a Computer Science major at the institution. The fact that the thumbnail was a girl that resembled her made her confide in the thought they would be friends if she attended, and she clicked it instantly.

After watching the video, it turned into watching another video. And then another video. And then another video. She didn't want to face the fact that her purpose of getting her laptop was to make progress on her application that would grant her access on the campus she worshiped.

Fear.

She thought about her dream of Simba and closed the video tab, now being faced with her perpetrator: her appeal application. She was on the essay portion, and it was still blank. She nearly felt offended it didn't write itself.

Sitting stagnant participating in a staring contest with it for nearly a lifetime, she closed her laptop shut abruptly, as the top and bottom flaps married aggressively. Her glasses began to fog up from her tears as she grew confused at the fact she couldn't devise a creative way to depict herself when she had done it successfully countless times in the past. Removing her glasses and placing them on her desk away from her, she sat upright on her bed and her little hands met her face in a face palm. Running away from her problems and failing to face them head-on was a recurring choice for her. She was an expert at this activity.

She had a fear of losing creativity.

Standing up and mentally instructing herself to gather herself together, she decided to have a conversation with her father. This always seemed like a great option when she was stressed out. Upon her arrival, he was seen typing rapidly on his laptop. Creativity clearly wasn't a roadblock on his path. He slowed down his pace as he directed his attention to her, acknowledging her with a glance.

"Dad, is college really that serious?"

Mr. Akintewe was thrown off by her bluntness. He grew familiar to her reserved nature of beating around the bush in most of their conversations with one another.

"Why do you ask that, sweetie?"

He folded his arms with a look of concern as he now gave her his undivided attention.

"It's just, I'm scared of it right now and that's just a local college. I can't even finish my UCLA application. And then that's UCLA so who knows if I'll even succeed there *if* I get in! And then—"

"Nia," he began, interrupting her. She knew when he called her by her government name he was being frank with her. "It isn't a good idea to be dumb, and obviously your mother and I believed in that, which is why she got her PhD and I got my Master's degree. It's important to invest in your education, no matter the vehicle you use to arrive at your destination."

She began listening to his words carefully, attempting to take it all in and analyze for herself if she agreed it was a necessity, given her fearful relationship with it.

"As a society, I feel we can blow the idea of college out of proportion and measure it higher than where it might need to be measured at because these institutions are all businesses and *do* view you as a check so I'll give you that. However, in society it's a good idea not to be dumb and be educated, and college just happens to be one convenient means of acquiring that knowledge.

"Quite frankly, after experiencing it and acquiring a couple degrees, I think the school system needs a rebrand. We reward students for getting things right or wrong. It's black and white. It's either a student chases that A and moves on, or they fail. I think that's a fixed mindset way of conducting school. It's an animalistic mindset of constantly battling to get good grades by any means, which doesn't focus on genuinely learning. Students have pressure to perform well and be viewed as desirable in the eyes of an institution that views them as a dollar. Isn't that weird? I think if we focused more on rewarding the fact that students may not have the answer instantly, it would promote more of a growth mindset in the education space. That's essentially promoting a mindset shift towards genuine effort if you ask me. The neurons in the brain make new stronger connections when students are getting smarter and genuinely want to learn. If we observe the brain activity of those that are in the fixed mindset education right now, we would see a difference in the two. There have been scientific studies conducted on this."

Nia took a moment to digest his statement. Realizing it was a powerful stance she felt addressed both sides and wasn't influenced with bias, she came to terms with the fact she could live with his opinion.

"Just don't attend college with the mentality to acquire thousands of dollars of debt just to get a job that's paying you $30,000 annually, because *that's* stupid and I won't allow you to do that. You're an Akintewe so start acting like it."

Nia was caught off guard. She never took the time to view college from a calculated manner in terms of what the institutions valued and how her approach should be. Besides the fact she just didn't want to deal with the time and stress of reapplying, she realized college was also a money game. Everyone had rent due on the 1st of the month.

"Nia, with everything I'm telling you, you have to feel me in your spirit! Like I always tell you, remember not to think having student loans for a long time is acceptable. I don't care what your classmates are telling you. It's a poison that our society has romanticized having over a long period of time. It's a cancer that'll always be lingering unless you attack it. Establish your relationship with money within your higher self. Your higher self is your spirit. It's the voice you hear talking when you don't talk. It's the voice one controls when they are meditating and operate on a high spiritual level. Communicate with your spirit.

Know your spirit. That's part of how I paid off my student loans quickly. Just stay with me.

"Most kid's brains haven't fully developed so they make the dumb decision of getting in high debt so I don't even blame the kids; I blame it on bad parenting. Regardless, I got you kiddo." He dished her with a playful pat on the back. "You just need to see a return on your investment and you're good to go, whether that be the knowledge that you can leverage to accumulate wealth or a degree from college that will give you the opportunity to make a considerable amount of money that's a return on your initial investment. Believe it, plan it out and execute it. It's that simple. Get a return on your investment. I repeated it for a reason."

Nia was elated she initiated this conversation with her father. He viewed the feeling of contentment coming from her big, beady brown eyes. He witnessed a new burning passion to succeed coming from her, and it couldn't have made him any prouder. He continued his spiel with passion.

"Nia baby, knowledge is important, because it's the beginning of someone being rich in spirit before they possess it in the physical form. With that knowledge, wisdom can be applied to plant the seeds into a successful fruition. That's something I need you to remember if you don't remember anything else I tell you. But don't let me talk your ear off, because you know when I start, I can go for hours."

"Oh I know Dad," Nia began, directing a devious smirk his way. "Once you start, we might be here for another three days! Who knows when you'll finish?"

"Hey, relax. But anyway, how are all your college applications coming along?"

Nia's heart raced rapidly like an individual who feared dogs was running away from a vicious pit bull. She tossed a confused look at him that made him reciprocate her expression.

"Applications? Applications as in plural?"

"Uh, yes ma'am. You want to transfer from your local community college and are applying to multiple schools aren't you?"

Nia looked down, avoiding eye contact with her father as she twiddled her thumbs, fidgeting nervously. He didn't chastise her for her insecurities so she glanced down this time solely out of fear of disappointing him.

"So actually, UCLA is the *only* school I'm applying to."

"Sweetie, I like the confidence you have in yourself, but you should definitely apply to more schools because it isn't smart to put all your eggs in one basket."

"Uh, it's not even about being confident, it's just because that's the only school I want to go to."

Her father's large right hand met his forehead as he took in what she had just told him. This was news to him.

"Nia, like I said it's not smart to put all your eggs in one basket. I'm not saying that you won't get into UCLA, because that's definitely a possibility with your entire application showcased effectively, but you need to be smarter about this."

"What do you mean?"

"I mean you *need* to have an abundance mindset. You can't live in fear that if you don't go to UCLA you should sabotage your entire academic career. It's always smart to have multiple plans instead of one for the fact that things don't always go as planned and everything isn't glitz and glamour how you envision it in your mind. The mind is a powerful thing you don't want to get fooled by. They say the average millionaire has several streams of income, so that's them exercising their freedom to have an abundance mindset. I want you to exercise your freedom to have an abundance mindset."

"So how do I do that if I don't want to go anywhere else? I'm just scared of this whole process and want it to be over with!"

"Let's try and take it easy. First, you need to come to terms with the fact that you're overhyping UCLA. Don't get me wrong, it's an amazing school, but it isn't the be all and end all if you don't go there. Don't place so much weight on it like there aren't any other comparable institutions you can attend. Second, I'm going to need you to do more research on other schools. I'm pretty sure you've done your research on UCLA from watching videos to dreaming about it."

Nia smiled wryly at the accuracy of her father's claims about the UCLA videos. She made her best effort to hide her emotions, and if her complexion permitted her the ability to blush, it would have been at this moment it would have occurred.

"I say that, because I don't want social media to influence your spirit negatively. I would even recommend you stay off social media so you don't get lost in others 'living' their lives. People only show their highlights on social media so it's easy to get caught up in that, think it's reality and fail. You want to focus on yourself and your goal only. The effect of social media has gotten worse year by year. It's crazy to think we're in 2025 and it's become even more infectious than it was five years ago. People live on there due to boredom. Focus!

"Most importantly sweetie, I need you to simply understand that wherever you're supposed to go, God will guide you there. You just have to believe. Don't lay stagnant though. An important trait to have with this college game though I've learned is having grit. And mastering it."

"I'm not even going to pretend like I know. What does grit mean?"

"It's essentially a trait of being resilient and having a strong character, and really important towards fostering a growth mindset. Remember growth mindset?"

"Yeah. That mindset you said I should have where I don't think my skills are just what they are and knowing I can improve. And you said I shouldn't have a fixed mindset."

"Exactly! We rebuke the spirit of a fixed mindset in all of us!" Her father put his hand up waiting for her to complete his high five. "But you shouldn't avoid a fixed mindset just because I said you shouldn't have one. You just shouldn't have one."

She rolled her eyes.

"Yeah, yeah Dad. You're right."

"Of course! No, but when you can master grit, you won't only succeed at college, but you'll achieve success at anything you want to accomplish in life."

There was utter silence. Her father knew there was something off about her. Nia disliked his ability to analyze her accurately when she didn't want to express herself, almost as much as she liked it when he accurately analyzed her when she craved his attention.

"Nia? Is anything else on your mind, dear? Anything that you're afraid of?" He gave her a quirky smile. "This is a free space to speak now or forever hold your peace."

"No." Her father analyzed her shift in energy. "I don't want to talk right now. I just want to take a nap. Later."

Nia returned back to her room in a jiffy. She felt contentment in her solitude at the moment. She often thought about the fact her problems often resulted in mood swings and she slightly felt guilty about how she answered her father, but it made her feel better momentarily. She stretched her body out on her bed and closed her eyes, daydreaming about her life at UCLA. She was in a circle of her college colleagues and they were all smiling having the best time of their lives. That was the life she desired without having to put in the hard work to get there. Within a couple of seconds, she was sound asleep.

Simba showed up once more. This time he glanced at her with a sense of urgency as if he had to get something off his chest he had been meaning to tell her for years.

"Ni Ni, all this fear. Your failed future-self allowed the failure of her driving test to be the driving force for her entire life and she let that control her. She didn't finish college or live any type of respectable life. She's now pitying herself and not taking responsibility for her actions. She was in a fixed mindset. *You* were in a fixed mindset. Is this the life you want to live?"

Nia felt placed in a defensive stance and grew emotional, as tears began streaming down her face.

"No! I don't. It's just hard because I can't get over my stupid fears!"

Simba sighed. "I'm not telling you to stop living in fear, you're human, but do your best to not be consumed by the fear. You can control that. Taking control of what you can control is the key. It's about taking control!" He clapped his hands aggressively. "Do your best!" He then shrugged, giving off his signature smirk Nia never forgot. "Is that not one of the four agreements?"

"Yes brother. It is. But why do you keep visiting me? Are you really here or I'm dreaming again?"

"Ni Ni, you're worried about the unnecessary. I'm here in this moment to give you wisdom and let you know I'm rooting for you. I'm not dead, I'm always with you wherever you are. I'm always thinking of you wherever you are."

Nia grew emotional to elevated levels she hadn't experienced since he passed away.

"So you just up and leave me like that?"

"You know it's not even like that. The one time I wanted to have fun in boring ol' Notsuoh, I get set up. I just couldn't deal with the money struggles and depression and I let it win the battle, which I regret. It was just crazy to me that Connor and Zane did me dirty like that. They were supposed to be my brothers. It really let me know you have to be careful with everyone around you, even family. Ni Ni, please promise me you'll focus on your goals and not veer off that path of focus, because I don't want what happened to me to happen to you. And never allow money to take control of your life. Deal?"

"I promised myself I wouldn't and I've been trying, but it's hard. I'm just always so scared of everything."

"What's your greatest fear?"

Nia was taken aback as she searched for an answer. After what felt like an eternity to come up with an answer, it hit her like a brick from a mile away.

"Being judged."

"Interesting. And why are you so worried about what others think about you?"

"I don't know man. That's just what it is. You asked me a question and I answered." She analyzed him and observed his distinct features once more, as tears started to well up, fogging her glasses. "Why did you have to go? You left me alone in this crazy ass world. Not you!"

He approached her and held her with a warm embrace.

"Ni Ni, stop crying. I know, I'm sorry."

"No!"

He let go and moved a few feet away to stand in front of her, hovering over her head as she stared up at him. As she took a moment to dry up her tears, he decided to ask her more questions before another stream of tears formed.

"Do you believe that you can get out of your situation?"

Nia rubbed her puffy eyes with her left hand, one at a time, clutching her glasses tightly in her right.

"What do you mean?"

"I mean, do you *believe* you can beat this fear? You said your greatest fear is being judged. You have a lot of insecurities. You're insecure about failing your written driving test. You're insecure about how you look. You're insecure about speaking, because of what happened to me, which hurts me *deeply*. I mean, do you *believe* you can overcome these fears?"

Nia shrugged.

"I guess I can overcome it."

"That doesn't sound like belief to me. Remember what Dad always says? If *you* don't even believe it, how is it going to work in the first place? If you don't believe yourself, how do you expect others to believe in you? You have to believe you'll get into UCLA. You have to believe you'll take control of your mind and your relationship with money and pay off your student loan debt. You have to feel that belief in your spiritual self. Like Dad told you, that's your higher self, or the inner voice you hear when you meditate or process thoughts. Work on these relationships and you'll excel out of this world. Most people aren't aware of this, and it took me losing my life as a sacrifice for me to learn it, and I think for you as well."

Nia fixed her gaze down at the ground.

"Okay."

"I'm one of your guardian angels, but I can't do the work for you. I'm a guardian. I can only protect you. It's up to you to *do*."

Nia opened her mouth in a surprised fashion.

"So you've been guarding me. I've been feeling your presence for a long time."

"Duh! But you should be upfront with Dad about your fears because that's how you'll get over it and take control. Communication is underrated. I really need you to remember this. Behind all that goofy joking around, you may not believe it, but he has some knowledge in that peanut head of his."

They laughed simultaneously as she wiped newly formed tears of contentment and hugged her brother with all her might.

"Brother, will I see you again?"

He let go of her and gave her a concerned look.

"I don't know...yet."

Poignant tears streamlined down her face rapidly, clogging her vision in the process as she stared at the silhouette that was once her brother. She wiped her tears as they formed, but they consistently replaced each other. After a minute of rubbing her eyes, she opened them.

She was awake and lost connection with her brother.

Fear.

Nia sat down for a moment attempting to recollect her thoughts and feelings of the dream as it started to depress her severely. She loved seeing Simba but didn't know if it was for the greater good, because she would wake up in a rut over the fact that he no longer existed in the physical form. She remembered distinctly what he said about being there for her.

I'm not dead, I'm always with you wherever you are. I'm always thinking of you wherever you are.

She sincerely hoped so. Smelling a beautiful aroma brewing in the kitchen, her stomach growled and she chased the smell. As she was about to arrive in the kitchen, she witnessed the orange hue she recognized to be Jollof Rice, a Nigerian delicacy.

Reconvening with him, she came to terms with the fact she was going to tell him about her dream. After all, the food smelled delicious, so she had to start a conversation with him somehow if she wanted a plate of this rice to complement her craving for goat meat.

"Dad, I had a dream about Simba."

Her father dropped the pan he was washing and stared at her with his mouth open.

"What?"

"I saw Simba in my dream. He was telling me about stuff and I got to thinking a bit." She fidgeted her fingers and avoided his eye contact, staring at the ground.

"Remember when I said I had nothing to say earlier? I actually have more stuff I'm afraid of."

He used a nearby hand towel to dry his hands and focused on Nia.

"Let's hear it."

Nia froze up and stared at her father in silence. She then animatedly displayed herself steering a wheel.

"Driving?"

She nodded her head, confirming his guess.

"Spill it out, we ain't got time to waste."

"I have a fear of driving. I mean look at my written test that I can't pass so I can't even drive a real car probably."

"You missed passing by one point. Don't let that deter you from the future. You're going to pass. What else?"

"I'm just stressed with a lot of things I have to do like college *applications,* as in plural now, and even your readings. I guess it's a therapy session now, huh?"

"You came to me so don't tell me never mind anymore. You have to break everything that you need to accomplish into parts so you don't overload your spirit and stress yourself out excessively. You shouldn't run away from your driving test, because it was only one mistake that stopped you from passing. You can start with that. Break everything down into simpler actionable steps. *That* will set you free from stress and overworking yourself."

She sighed aggressively.

"I guess you are right."

"Anything else?"

"My greatest fear. My greatest fear is being judged. I *hate* being made fun of for my lack of composure when it comes to speaking, because I keep thinking about that day at the funeral when we buried Simba."

He pat her on her head, running his fingers through her natural hair she desired to conceal.

"This is news to me!" He sighed. "But I know sweetie, it's tough. You have to maximize your insecurities though."

Nia was befuddled.

"Maximize...my...insecurities? Simba mentioned that in the dream!"

"Oh wow. But yes baby. Maximize your insecurities."

"How exactly do I do that?"

Her father smiled and his posture shifted into a more energetic one.

"Okay, it's a teaching moment now! This is a topic I speak about during my motivational speeches, so I'll let you in on a little secret because people pay thousands of dollars to hear this. Don't forget, I used to be afraid of public speaking too, so let me tell you how I maximized that insecurity."

"Okay."

"When I was in college, my friends knew I was scared of public speaking and I would place bets with one of them about volunteering first to give speeches in class or wherever. If I didn't volunteer to do it or if any other speaking opportunity came up and I didn't do it, I would owe him $20 each time I fumbled the opportunity, but he would give me $10 when I didn't. I got tired of being scared and losing money and eventually kept stepping up and got great at speaking over time through experience. I used my insecurity as advantageous fuel."

"Wow Dad! I never knew that about you. That's actually a little bit inspiring. I didn't think you would ever go through something like that."

"Yeah, we all have our problems sweetie. Remember though, growth mindset might seem easy since we talk about it a lot, but most people do a lot of talking and not a lot of doing."

"That's true!"

"I'm going to give you another tool to calm your nerves, and I mentioned it briefly before, but this tool is meditation. I want to gift you with this special tool that is so dear to me, because it helped me take control of my stress with speaking. When you were younger you used to meditate with me, but would laugh and go running off somewhere else in the middle of our sessions. I'm going to recommend you get back to it because it's a powerful tool that takes control of your spiritual and mental battles. You can even argue it takes control of the physical.

Nia appeared interested.

"How so?"

"You're in tune with your inner self or higher self while meditating for your spiritual psyche, because that voice in your head you hear when you aren't talking is your spirit. It's also a mental battle to be able to sit still for a long time. It's practicing the ability to shut up. A lot of people do too much talking and should shut up and meditate." They both laughed. "As for the physical, meditation can physically heal you. That's another thing. There's meditation and then there's medication."

Her father put both his hands up, his left hand lower and his right hand higher.

"In my left hand right here is medication. This is all the drugs and self-medication people use to cope with their problems. This is the fixed mindset."

He moved his right hand slightly to direct her attention to it.

"In my right hand here is meditation. This is the thing where we focus on our breathing and forget about all our problems in the world. This is the growth mindset. You following me still?"

"Yeah."

"So they are two very similar words, but different entities, and the difference is just a substitution of one letter. The difference between the two is that medication is associated with those people living in a fixed mindset and meditation is associated with those living in a growth mindset. What do you want?"

"Growth mindset. Meditation."

"Exactly! The difference between someone that has a growth mindset and someone that has a fixed mindset is the person that has a growth mindset knows their self! The person with a fixed mindset does not know their self! You following me?"

"Yeah!"

"The difference between someone that has a growth mindset and someone that has a fixed mindset is the person with a growth mindset *knows* who they are, while the fixed mindset person is lost and *does not know* who they are. I need to repeat it for your understanding. We're *rebuking* the spirit of a fixed mindset!

"It becomes quite simple. So if you see, my left hand is lower and my right hand is higher. Lower is medication and fixed mindset and that's 50%, because they aren't operating at their full potential. My right hand is meditation and growth mindset and that's 190%, because they are operating at their full potential."

"Why 190%?"

Her father smirked as if he anticipated this exact question.

"Because that's *nearly* twice as good as our best effort. I'll touch on that later. Anyway, when it comes to conquering your fears, you have to first believe in your soul that you'll overcome it. *That's* the spiritual aspect of the power of overcoming!"

Nia sighed obnoxiously, alerting her father as he thought something was wrong with her.

"What happened?"

"That's pretty much what Simba was telling me in my dream. He said I have to believe in myself, so it's just crazy you're saying the same thing. I'm starting to believe it's true."

Her father laughed as he pushed his glasses up with his left index finger.

"You're starting to *believe* it's true. That's a nice pun!"

"Uh, I didn't do that on purpose, but thanks?"

"Oh, that's fine. But I'm going to put you on some more game, baby girl. You should have three types of friends: mentor, peers and there's one more. I'll be your mentor. It's important that you recognize women in technological fields, like the Computer Science field you want to pursue, tend to lack mentors compared to their male counterparts. What I'm doing for you right now is really pivotal to your development and I want you to know that."

"Thanks Dad! Yeah I definitely see the difference in treatment at school, and that's part of why I want to give up a lot of the time, because not only am I a woman in this space, but I'm a black woman, so it's double the trouble and it's just disheartening sometimes."

"Exactly! And oftentimes in many situations of representation, black women are an afterthought, so it's important to be intentional about protecting the black woman especially when it comes to technological aspirations where the representation is thinner than a piece of paper. It's important to recognize that, *but* don't let that be a determinant in deterring you from performing exceptionally. I don't want you to focus on excuses. Either way, I got your back!"

"Thanks Dad!"

"No problem. I need you to know: you *will* be tested. Your coworkers and classmates will congratulate you for what you think is minimal work accomplished. You'll then wonder if you've actually accomplished something notable or if they're just raising the bar low for you which is obviously subtle disrespect. Persevere and work twice as hard. Work so hard you no longer have to introduce yourself." He paused dramatically. "You're not listening sweetie. Work hard enough that you no longer have to introduce yourself! This doesn't mean work excessively because sometimes working harder means working smarter.

"I fully believe in mentorship in my spirit, which is why I think it's important to bring all this to your attention. Black women are obviously still underrepresented in these fields, but that's only for today. Having the growth mindset of the expansion of black women in technology is very powerful, and it starts with you as an aspiring Computer Scientist! I want you to read this book and we'll discuss the last type of friend."

Nia read the title as he displayed it for her eyes to feast on.

"*Mentor: The Kid and The CEO*? Why can't you just tell me what the last one is?"

"Just read the book and we'll discuss it."

Nia sighed dramatically.

"Fine."

He handed her the book.

"Work on recruiting a peer that's walking in the same path as you as well and we'll discuss the book. You're a quick reader, and it's an easy quick one so I'll give you one week. Understood?"

"Understood!"

"Alright, good night Daddy."

Nia expressed her fond adieu to her father for the night, thinking she would capture a good night's rest immediately. As soon as her body met her bed, she quickly realized she had alternative plans. She rose up to turn her light back on and began reading Tom Pace's *Mentor: The Kid and the CEO*. A couple pages in and she was hooked!

3

SUCCESS BECAUSE...

"Thank God it's Monday!"

Nia heard her father in the living room yelling in unison with motivational speaker, Eric Thomas. She glanced at her phone to see a bright 3:00 AM flashing on her phone screen, nearly blinding her in the process. Confused, she clicked the snooze button and went back to sleep instantly, cognizant of the fact she needed to be up at 6:30 AM to get ready and be at school by 7:30 AM. Her routine for school was sitting in her bed for 15 minutes on her phone, taking a shower and brushing her teeth for another 15 minutes, using 15 minutes to put her clothes on and eat breakfast, and the last 15 minutes was reserved for her father driving her to the battlefield.

In the blink of an eye, her alarm rang and it now read 7:00 AM. Nia was in panic mode. She was so shocked, she didn't know how to react immediately and sat in place for five minutes, before realizing she had only 25 minutes to spare before she had to be at school. She stood up and ran to her bathroom and quickly attempted to put toothpaste on her brush after initially wetting it. The toothpaste fell off her brush and she attempted again, finally accomplishing the toothpaste meeting her toothbrush. Aggressively attacking her mouth, she turned the shower water to its highest level and calculated she had 10 minutes to do everything if they were to leave on time.

"2 minute brushing, 3 minute shower, and 5 minutes to put my clothes on and eat breakfast. Okay!"

She quickly ejected the saliva and toothpaste combination from her mouth, rinsed once more and let out a minty sigh. Hopping in the shower, she slipped and fell to the ground, landing on her back, making a loud, potent sound.

"Come on!"

"Everything good in there sweetie?"

"Yeah I'm fine Dad! I'll be out soon!" She quickly rose up and lowered her dialogue to herself. "How did he even hear me and he's doing all that yelling?"

"You said what sweetie?"

"Nothing!" She quickly turned her head and focus back towards her shower and scrubbed herself quickly. "Nosy."

In nearly seconds, she was out of the shower and dressed in her signature yellow hoodie and out in the kitchen reunited with her father.

"I heard a loud noise and I had to make sure you were doing okay. You alright?"

"Yeah Dad, I said it's nothing, I'm fine. I'm just so tired!" She glanced at the time, stretching her arms upward. It read: 7:29. "We gotta go Dad! Come on and hurry up! You wanna always ask so many questions!" Grabbing an apple, she rushed past her father to the car.

As the car ride started, after nearly getting to the core of her apple and Travis Scott's "Sicko Mode" reaching its ending, Nia broke the silence.

"Dad, I need to tell you something."

"You want to talk about the book?"

"No, that's not what I wanted to bring up."

"Spill it out then."

"I have a fear of failure, because I'm afraid of being judged."

"Okay? You told me that already."

She ignored him.

"I have a fear of failure, because I'm afraid I'm going to fail my written driving test again."

"Okay? Again you told me that."

She ignored him once more.

"I have a fear of failure, because I'm afraid I won't get accepted into UCLA and you'll disown me and I'll disappoint the family."

He realized she was being vulnerable and decided to let her get her soapbox off.

"I have a fear of failure, because I don't know if I'll ever get over my fear of public speaking. I have a fear of failure, because I'm afraid I'll get used to it and accept that as my norm. I have a fear of failure, because I'm scared of my insecurities controlling my mind. I have a fear of failure, because I'm scared I'll misuse my financial aid."

Nia took a deep breath and sighed aggressively. "I don't know what got into me or what that apple did to me, but I had to get that off my chest. I feel like I have a brain fart now because I had a thought and now I lost it."

"It's because we're in the car probably."

A light bulb lit up in Nia's head.

"Now that I think about it, I always get brain farts when we're in the car for a certain amount of time. I feel like my ideas flow when I'm outside of the car."

"It's the idea of being marginalized in a box. You probably fear failure, because you don't want to be marginalized in a box since that makes you seem simple. When we are in a box, we fit any label that someone imposes on us and we don't have control. We don't have the full range to operate."

"But I feel good though."

He oscillated his hand. "Look around. We're in a car which is safe from the outside world on the surface, or safe from judgments and stuff, which is why we are comfortable to be ourselves. However..." He placed his hand up, wiggling his index finger. "And this is a big however...there's also an element of disconnect even though you can see other people in the other cars."

Nia glanced at her father in disbelief with her mouth wide open.

"You're too deep for me Dad, but if you say so. You sound like one of those crazy J. Cole fans or something!"

"You're crazy!" He laughed aggressively. "But I have a question!"

"What?"

"Who are you and who am I?"

"I'm Nia Akintewe, and you're my father who loves me!"

"What do you deserve?"

"I deserve all the love in the world!"

"What are the three pillars for financial freedom to get rid of your student loan debt or overcome anything you encounter?"

"Believe. Plan. Execute."

"Why should you practice patience?"

"Patience allows me to take risks without repercussions because it gives me the mindset to focus on the fact that I have time."

"And why is gratitude so important?"

"You can't be great without being grateful, it's in the word if you reverse the letters."

They drove in silence as the radio was the only sound heard in the car for several minutes. They arrived at her school and as Nia stepped out, she began to feel like she had to break the silence again and began her attempt to talk, but quickly stopped. Her father noticed and turned the radio all the way down.

"Yeah sweetie?"

"I have a fear of failure, because I'm not only afraid of disappointing others, but I'm afraid of disappointing myself."

"It won't be easy trust me, but you just have to change your way of thinking and realize that failure is a state of mind. It's very important when mastering the growth mindset. It won't be done in one day, but when you have that belief, that's the foundation of your successful execution!"

"Okay Dad," she began, staring down. "I'm just scared of failure, because I just don't know if I should believe that everything will turn out good."

"Timothy 4:10 says 'That is why we labor and strive, because we have put our hope in the living God, who is the Savior of all people, and especially of those who believe' which sounds crystal clear to me. Believe! It's about the power of the spirit! Not only that, failure is a state of mind and you must remember that success is going to be an iterative process. It won't be accomplished on the first rodeo. Chase that failure so you can succeed. You *should* want to fail! *Focus,* so you can *fail!* *Fail,* so you can *focus.* Fall down 30 times and get back up 31!"

Nia wasn't comprehending the value her father provided her, because she was in a fixed mindset. She began rolling her eyes while thinking of a new topic to divert the attention of the conversation elsewhere.

She displayed a fictitious smile.

"You got a new read for me yet, old man?"

Her father quickly picked up on what she was attempting to do.

"To answer your question about the books," he began, laughing. "I see you've gotten into a rhythm of reading the books I recommend you. I told you that you're disciplined, you just had to *believe it* from me telling you and now look. You sought that validation from me and that allowed you to execute."

Nia stared at him in disbelief. He proved she had underlying spirit of belief about her. She failed to recognize that within herself, because she focused her mind on the wrong things. Shrugging and placing a finger on her chin, she thought about how she was now starting to become more spiritual as a result of witnessing her evolution into a self-disciplined individual blooming right before her own eyes.

"I know you're amazed Nia, but I have experience being a coach. I simply made you realize how to unlock the potential you already had. That's what I do with my financial coaching for my clients. But I actually know the perfect book you can read next. It'll help you with how you're viewing failure since that's key for you right now. Have you finished the mentor book?"

She struggled to answer.

"Yeah I did," she stated, lying through the gap in her teeth.

"Okay? So what are the three types of friends you should have?"

"Um, I would have to go back and make sure."

"If you lie to me about it or not, you're only hurting yourself. Another thing is so many people blindly read and don't apply what they're reading. So I encourage you as you *actually* read, don't focus on speed reading these books, because quite frankly, I would rather have you be in the mindset that you're focused on how to apply page three to your life instead of being on page 259 and you ain't applied nothing."

"Wow, that's true! I usually speed read because I get so excited if it's really good!"

"Yup. If you continue to do that, given that I just told you that's an issue, you're continuing to choose to live in a fixed mindset. You represent our brand so I'm going to need you to rebuke that spirit of a fixed mindset and come over to this side of a growth mindset and be delivered!"

Nia appeared sad. She felt guilty for lying. Regardless of whether or not her father knew she was lying, she wasn't about to expose herself. Picking up on her sad gaze, her cuteness always got to him. Whenever she had her signature sad demeanor, she could ask her father for anything in the world and she would receive it easily. This time wasn't about manipulation, it was genuine guilt. She made a promise to him to keep the brand strong and he sighed, observing her.

"I guess I can tell you about the new book. I want you to know that I want you to focus on school though, because that's a priority and comes first. Understood?"

"Understood. Tell me!"

Her father magically retrieved a book from under his driver's seat.

"Think!"

"Think about what?"

"...and Grow Rich!"

"Huh? And grow rich?"

"That's the title of the next book you should read. It's by Napoleon Hill. *Think and Grow Rich*. This is a life changing book for many around the world, including myself. I actually have told you about it in little conversations in the past, but you might not remember. I try and read it annually just to refresh myself on the principles. I want you to specifically really focus on this one for a while because this is an important one! This is my copy though. I'll give you yours later."

Nia did recall the name of the book as a familiar one that her father told her was dear to his heart, because he told her mother about it, as they read and discussed its principles. She was spectacular at reading her father and immediately picked up on the passion in which he spoke about the book. His eyes lit up as she noticed his illustrated hand oscillations and knew this book was something that she would want to dive into.

As Nia still stood in place heeding her father's words, he realized he was holding her up from going to her class. Scanning the surroundings he quickly apologized to her and encouraged her to go to class.

"Look at you standing up right now. We all failed as babies and failed to stand up for a long period of time, but you're doing it now. This is what I mean when I talk about growth mindset and fixed mindset. As babies, we had a growth mindset because we didn't care about falling and focused on failing until we reached that ounce of success. Babies are geniuses man! Alright sweetie!"

"Bye Dad!"

Nia took out her earphones from the pouch of her hoodie, inserted them in her ears and played the first song that was immediately in her music queue. The phone started playing "Goosebumps" by Travis Scott. She accepted she no longer related to the song of her love interest giving her goosebumps as she walked courageously to the entrance of the campus, ready to take on any obstacles that crossed her path.

"I hope no one makes fun of my natural hair today," she thought to herself as she sported her afro and placed her hood conveniently on top of her head.

She began getting deep into her thoughts as the music played. The rapid upbeat tempo was making her heart race and recall the moment in time when she had experienced fainting from giving her speech. She then thought about the fact her father told her to recruit a peer walking in the same path as her. She felt weird about it, because she didn't want to be perceived as a nerd for this odd request.

Walking into her math class, she took a seat reluctantly. She knew the results from the test they took the previous week would be handed out. She took out her water bottle and sat next to an acquaintance she often saw in a majority of her classes. It was a boy that had been trying to capture her attention since the class went over the syllabus on the first day. He was extremely tall and overweight, built like a bear. He was slightly lighter than Nia in complexion and had noticeably crooked teeth.

She still didn't know his name to this day and he wanted to be her friend more than she wanted to be his; she wasn't completely sure if his intentions were purely friendly. Nia felt a weird energy about him deep in her spirit. She noticed him staring at her in her peripheral vision and she replayed "Goosebumps" and bumped up the volume to the max potential, thinking that would stop him from making an attempt to talk to her. That didn't stop him as she saw him mouthing words she couldn't make out and she took off her earphones in an annoyed fashion.

"Hey Nia!"

"I'm right here. What do you want?"

"Oh, your music was so loud I didn't even know if you could hear me."

She stared at him agitated.

"Okay, so what do you want?"

He appeared nervous. A large boy that resembled that of a bear was disempowered by what seemed to be a small, fragile girl on the surface. Because she was a black girl, by nature she inevitably endured countless obstacles at any given time that prepared her for eventually being a strong black woman; this scenario became a conceivable action.

"I...do you like 'Goosebumps' with Travis and Kendrick?"

"Yes."

Nia inserted her earphones back in her ears. She waited for the icing on the cake for the damage to be done when she received her test results. The boy received his test and let out a celebratory sigh, pumping his fist in the air. Nia glanced at him with her mouth open, disgusted at the fact he either performed extremely well or his standards were set extremely low to the point he was satisfied. She continuously drank water as she grew nervous and her mouth grew parched. She was handed her test as the professor folded the paper to keep the confidentiality of her score. She felt the spirit of eventual Computer Science achievement leaving her body. Her heart raced as she attempted to grab the paper from her hand, but she fumbled it and it went flying across the lecture hall nearly to the front of the hall, like a paper airplane on its way to its landing ground, many feet away from its departing point.

Embarrassed, Nia rose up quickly from her seat and retrieved the paper, as her hood separated from the top of her head as she received countless stares. If she could blush, this would be the moment where her skin would be flushed. Returning back to her seat with her paper in hand, she still wasn't certain how she performed on the test. Sitting down, she took another sip out of her water bottle and glanced around to search for any nearby eyewitnesses creeping over her shoulders. The coast was clear and she finally observed her score.

61.9%.

"Damn it!"

The entire class focused on her as she realized she let out a bellowing obscenity. Another potential blushing moment, she acted as if nothing occurred and retrieved her phone, pretending to scroll through something, as she scrunched her face like she read some alarming news. She was praying the class average was as low as her score. That was the only thing that could save her now. At this point, she could say goodbye to her UCLA dreams.

She heard the boy clear his throat. She immediately rolled her eyes anticipating his words to annoy her.

"What did you get Nia?"

Without glancing at him or moving a centimeter, she replied right on time.

"A test."

"You're funny! Black girl magic huh? Okay, I guess you probably got like a C or something then."

"I wish," she muttered to herself.

"What was that?"

"Nothing."

The professor informed the class of their exceptional performance on a general basis. She stated the highest score was 105% due to extra credit offered whereas the lowest score was 61.9%. The boy laughed and nudged Nia.

"I wonder who got that 51.2%, huh Nia? Did they even study?"

"It was 61.9%, but yeah. I wonder who."

Nia began criticizing herself on the inside and doubting her ability to amount to anything during her lifetime. She started falling in deep thought thinking Kosey was accurate with his slander towards her. After many negative thoughts and existing in the dark depths of despair, she quickly realized she hated failure, because she let it define who she was. She also thought about the fact her father told her to recruit a peer on the same path as her, but she feared rejection. Not only did she fear rejection, but in her eyes, she feared that everyone was already ahead of her and she was playing catch up.

The class transitioned into a lecture for new material. Nia barely followed along. Taking notes sporadically, she thought about failure and its clutch on her as she grew nauseous and fidgety. She was cognizant that she partially had a fear of failure, because she was a perfectionist with everything she aspired to do, delicately always checking her answers numerous times on her tests and conducting the same checking process with her notes. She began to hear whispers around her.

"That natural hair she has is so unprofessional," one voice stated.

"Yeah, look at her. She needs to put on a wig or something," another voice stated.

Nia ignored them as she placed her hood on top of her head once more and began self-sabotaging her experience in class. She crossed out lines in her notes, writing 'UCLA' randomly all over her margins. She wanted an excuse to not perform to the best of her ability so it wasn't that she simply failed. She wanted the narrative to be that she experienced failure, because she was a former perfectionist operating out of her element since her notes were so messy; she would conveniently not take accountability for her shortcomings.

Class ended and she immediately rose aggressively, leaving the classroom to the bathroom to view herself. She began cursing herself out in the mirror, frustrated at her life. What would she do with her life? How would she get to UCLA and continue what Simba started? How would she not destroy the legacy of her family's beginnings?

"Everyone is ahead of me, so who am I to ask someone to be a peer of mine when *they* could be my mentor?"

She took time to wipe the tears that clouded her vision. Glancing towards the entrance/exit of the bathroom, she didn't notice or hear anyone approaching and continued her critique of herself.

"You're so selfish! Simba is gone! He doesn't exist anymore and you have the nerve to get a 61.9% on your test? What do you think Dad is gonna think of you? I really am scared of failure, because I let these stuff define me." She lodged a closed fist at the surface of the sink's counter like a judge's gavel meeting its sound block following a decision. "I hate it!"

Nia took a long look at herself in the mirror once more.

"I'm a short, four-eyed crazy girl crying and talking to myself in the mirror. This is what my life has come to? I've got low self-esteem and I'm afraid of being my authentic self in front of people that don't know me, so I put up a front *not* to be judged. I'm a perfectionist and got 61.9% on my math test. I'm also scared to take a risk because I might succeed and self-sabotage myself since I won't know how to handle that success. I'm also scared of success because I don't know how people would act around me if I got it. I really have a fear of success more than failure."

Nia laughed as she glanced over at the entrance/exit once more and redirected her vision at her reflection again.

"I'm...crazy!"

She laughed hysterically at herself and wiped the tears again, feeling slightly better after crying the situation off.

"I guess sometimes you just have to cry it off."

She retrieved her worn backpack and spirit. As she proceeded to walk out the bathroom door, within the blink of an eye it was like everything after her judgment of herself happened so quickly that she was now back at home with a headache from crying.

Nia was confused.

"That was a quick Monday today. I guess thank God it is Monday?"

"Always sweetie! Always."

Her father's presence startled her and she wondered why she didn't recollect what occurred after her tirade in the bathroom. She quickly asked her father what he was doing. He was amused.

"Look around, this is the living room. You've been really tired ever since you came home. You looked *really* tired when I picked you up and then you threw your backpack on the ground right there and knocked out here in the living room. We've got to get you a new backpack by the way. But why don't you go to your room and rest for your driving test tomorrow?"

Nia didn't recall any of this, as the last thing she recalled was crying in the bathroom. She rose up, collected her slandered backpack and retreated to her room to sleep on her luxurious bed. She was confused as to why it wasn't her initial choice for a sleeping surface when she first arrived home. Marrying her top and bottom eyelids on both eyes, she was fast asleep.

Nia was now surrounded by an unfamiliar atmosphere. Her vision was clear, but it was blurry to a certain degree. It appeared to be a cold area, but she felt warm. It all didn't make sense to her. Glancing around, she noticed she was in the midst of a beautiful area. It was a completely blue radiant area with sparkling residue that tricked the human eye. She felt like she was submerged in the deepest abyss of the ocean and it was beautiful without all the sea creatures one could imagine.

Panicking, she took a deep breath to confirm she wasn't in an ocean. The coast was clear.

Easy breathing.

Tranquility.

She felt like her spirit was at ease in a meditative state. She was in her sanctuary now. Her only worry now was that she was the only person in this region. She went from being surrounded by many people and feeling metaphorically alone, to now being literally alone and began to panic once more.

"Hello!" She yelled with an alarmingly high inflection of a goddess.

As she yelled out in her pursuit to find more companions, she heard her echo loud and clear. Fascinated by what she heard, she continued once more, increasing the inflection in her voice.

"Hello! Is anybody there?"

"You called for somebody?"

Nia immediately jumped back as she heard the whistling whisper in her ear. Her armpits grew itchy as she scanned her surroundings once more, observing a beautiful woman. She had a similar sounding voice to hers. Familiar sounding voice to videos her father would show her sporadically when he traveled down memory lane. Nia immediately knew who it was when she laid her eyes on her and observed her distinct features that both of them shared. She gazed at her radiant skin that was controversially a weapon.

It was her mother!

"Mommy!"

Nia jumped at her and embraced her so tightly she nearly began to hurt her.

"It's very good to see you sweetie, but you know this is a dream and when you wake up, you'll be back to reality."

Nia stared at her in awe attentively, taking in each and every word she said, attempting to experience every breath her mother took. She analyzed the way her mother's lips moved, fascinated. This was the first time she dreamt of her mother, and in Nia's eyes, it was a random isolated event for her to meet her now.

"By the way, that boy in your class inserted a rapid dissolving drug into your water bottle when you left your seat to go and grab your math test after it flew to the front of the classroom. I wasn't sure if you picked up on that. I'm just glad nothing worse happened. Please Nia, our time is precious, but don't leave anything of yours unattended, especially around these predatory monsters."

Nia's heart raced. It all made sense now. This was why she didn't remember her father picking her up after crying in the bathroom. She felt content her mother was able to bring this to her attention, but also felt slightly embarrassed. Her mother witnessed her crying spiel.

"Don't be embarrassed. I'm your other guardian angel. I've always been watching you sweetheart, but I decided to finally reveal myself because you're mature enough to grasp what I want to tell you."

"Okay, I'm listening. This is just so crazy, because I've seen videos of you, but never got to meet you so I don't know how to react right now. Part of me wants to cry and part of me is just shaking right now, holding in my emotions!"

"Sweetie, I know you feel that way, but I've always been with you wherever you were so I don't feel like this is our first time meeting. I also held you in my arms before I left physically. I named you Nia for a reason." Nia's mother grew emotional in the same manner Nia did, as sparkling tears meandered down her clear mahogany skin; Nia observed an angelic aura surrounding her as her words now carried more weight. "Your name means purpose in Swahili Nia. You exist for a purpose and I'm going to need you to do better."

Nia's heart raced once more as she felt the novel feeling of being lectured by her mother for the first time.

"What do you mean Mama?"

Her mother snapped her fingers potently and instantly a woman appeared between both of them. This individual was noticeably senior to Nia, but younger than her mother and resembled both of them. However, she appeared disheveled. She seemed like she didn't care about herself and was on the verge of losing hope to continue living. The mystery woman maintained her back facing Nia's mother as she stared into Nia's big beady eyes, with her low, hopeless eyes.

Nia's mother closed her eyes and tilted her head down as she placed her right hand on the woman's shoulder. A contrast was observed as the luminescent aura emitted from her mother's hand was easily distinguishable on the mystery woman's shoulder. Nia's mother spoke.

"Nia darling. This is your failed future-self if you don't do better and take control of your life like I've kindly requested."

"Mom, what do you mean by your request exactly?"

"Nia, a star can only shine in darkness."

"Mom?"

"Without the student loan epidemic that's been unfortunately normalized, you wouldn't be able to appreciate applying the knowledge and wisdom you shall gain to pay it off quickly. When you get your financial aid money, take advantage of it by *not* spending it uselessly. You need to have the mindset that you're paying more than you borrowed back. What you're borrowing will be paid back in more than you initially borrowed due to interest, so manage your money right *now* and start investing and saving immediately!

"It's up to you to apply that knowledge though. You can focus and succeed, or lay stagnant and fail. The fact that there's a degree of normalcy to paying off one's debts forever rather than sooner is mind-boggling to me. Please listen closely."

Her voice slowly faded away, as she disappeared slowly. It was like she was being shredded to beautiful, shiny smithereens.

Nia panicked.

"Mama!"

Nia's failed future-self peered over her shoulder to observe the remnants of the sparkling dust from her mother's dissolve. She fixed her gaze on Nia.

"I don't want you to end up like me," she began, capturing Nia's attention instantly, sounding exactly like Nia's current self. Despite aging, it was as if her voice didn't change over time simply because she didn't progress in life. "You're me, but I'm not you, if that makes sense. A lot of time has passed between us and I wish I could go back in time and fix it all up. You need to view difficult differently. That's a concept I wish I understood when I was a college freshman, or when I was you."

"What do you mean by view difficult differently?"

"I mean that you, or I, should have the mindset where you look at things you find difficult in the same light as things you enjoy. We love reading books. We didn't view things like our driving test and transferring to UCLA or any college in that same positive light when we should have. It's not just that. I've encountered so many other things that made me depressed, but I'm using that as an example. I remember that's what we were struggling with at this time."

"Yeah, that's interesting."

"I don't want you to end up like me. Your story is still fixable and you have to listen to Dad when he talks all that growth mindset and fixed mindset stuff. I know it gets annoying, but he knows what he's talking about...a little bit." They chuckled together. "I don't want you to end up like me, because that's the path you're heading towards currently and it makes me sad. It really doesn't have to be that way. You have the chance to have the right mindset to achieve your goals and even graduate with paid off student loans if you start from the spirit. Look, you see that light over there?"

Nia's vision traveled the path of her older self's finger. She was nearly blinded as her eyes met a shining light. She scrunched her face, going from squinting aggressively to looking away.

"I see it, but what's that light?"

"Look closer now." The light dimmed as Nia laid her eyes on an angelic silhouette that shined as bright as her mother's. "That's the successful version of yourself that did what I wish I did when I was you right now."

Nia grew excited as her disgust for boys disappeared temporarily.

"Is she married?"

Nia's failed future-self chuckled. "I can't spoil your story for you, but if you want to become that radiant, successful queen standing over there, you must listen to me and right our wrongs. Be confident and don't live in a fixed mindset anymore. Rebuke the spirit of a fixed mindset! You can do it. Don't say you can't do it."

"Thank you for the encouragement. Or should I thank myself instead?" Nia inquired, amused at her own joke.

"No! Don't be like me. Be like her! She's so radiant and successful, we can't even stand near her. We can only see her in the distance and admire her beauty and black excellence."

"Got it. I'll definitely keep that in mind and get rid of the fixed mindset in my spirit. How do I do that though besides just agreeing I will? I read *The Four Agreements* so I'm familiar with words and trying to follow them but I don't know. I just fear failure, because..."

"I'm afraid of being judged," they stated simultaneously.

"I know this already Nia! I'm the *failed* future version of yourself! And you fear success for the same reason! We fear success because we don't want people to ask us for things and feel entitled to our success."

Nia feared success because she didn't want those around her to feel entitled to her success. Nia feared success because she had been abused verbally countless times to the point she internalized that feedback and assumed she didn't deserve success. She didn't want those around her to start asking for things they wouldn't normally ask for, because her paranoia told her that was an inevitable occurrence with success. She didn't want those closest to her to change how they treated her prior to her ascent. She didn't want her 'friends' to be jealous of her and plan out a ploy that would lead to her demise, like they did to Simba. She didn't want envious energy around her, but that was a byproduct of success. She wasn't spiritually equipped to take control of these spiritual battles and handle perpetrators to her success, so she simply shoved success away from herself, allowing others to claim it. If she knew she was leading a race, she would self-sabotage her potential success to finish last. Her fear of success trumped her fear of failure by a large margin.

"But to answer your question about what you need to do, you need a spiritual cleansing; you need to take control of your spirituality in this spiritual phase of your life. You need a spiritual awakening! You're dealing with these insecurities and inconsistencies in your life of being unsure about where you're headed, because you need to work on your relationship with God!"

"How do you know that?"

"I'm the future version of yourself Nia. I wasn't successful because of my mindset currently, but I still had a pure mindset when I was you. Trust me, Nia. I was you at one point. I remember this exact time in your...our life."

"Okay. I'm done questioning you. I fully trust you."

"Good. You need to perform a 21-day fast."

Nia reacted dramatically.

"21 days...fast? As in no food whenever I want for 21 days?"

"I didn't stutter Nia. You need to prioritize your relationship with God and maximize your spiritual strength while practicing discipline. You have a lot going on in your life, and a lot of negative demons, so we need to rebuke and cleanse them out of your system and spirit if you want to succeed and do something admirable like pay off your debts quickly. That's something I didn't do that Mrs. Shiny Angel over there did. This helped her build her spiritual strength and take control of her spirituality and satisfy one piece of the puzzle for having a growth mindset. There are three pieces in total."

"You said Mrs. as in she's married! So *I am* married in the future? Just tell me!"

"No Nia, you're missing the point!"

"No? You said no! So I'm not married in the future with two daughters living in a huge mansion, driving an expensive car and wearing a lot of different wigs?"

"I didn't say that. I said you're missing the point. Do you want to be her or me?"

 Nia chuckled.

"I didn't mean to laugh, I'm sorry. That just came off funny to me. No disrespect, but I want to be her. You can continue."

"Nia listen closely. This is something I didn't understand."

"I'm all ears."

"The main lesson of this 21-day exercise isn't to harm yourself. If you can control something as simple as your eating habits you will have no problem controlling any other aspect in your life. Being able to control that means you're equipped to pay off your student loans easily. You're eager for Dad to teach you about finances so you can pay off whatever student loans you get. It starts with this!

"You must also understand the consequences of having student loans forever. You have to understand this first. I wish I knew this early on because it would have helped with my discipline of doing that UCLA transfer appeal. Not only appealing that, but it also would have helped me with just the belief I'd be accepted where I was supposed to be, regardless of where it was."

"Did you transfer successfully?" Nia caught herself. "Actually never mind you can't tell me future stuff."

"You're learning quickly." Her failed future-self smirked. "So like I said, perform that 21-day fast and you'll see the results and after that, things will be much clearer. Following taking control of your spirit to help overcome future spiritual battles, you'll want to take control of the mental phase in your life. That's the second piece where you'll be financially literate. After taking control of that to overcome future mental battles, you'll want to take control of the physical phase. That's the final puzzle piece you'll need for having a growth mindset. The knowledge base for paying off your student loans quickly is predicated off of having a growth mindset so embrace this mindset. You'll need three tools to overcome each of these phases. "

"You're giving me weapons or what do you mean by tools?"

"No. I already talked about one of them, but you'll need to apply discipline like I discussed, consistency and effort towards all three of those phases. It's called the Rule of Nine. Remember that, but don't think about it too much. Just remember the three phases are spiritual, mental and physical."

"Okay. I understand."

"Excellent. Once that's done, you've fulfilled your requirements and I have no worry that you'll have a growth mindset and possess the tools necessary to accomplish anything you set your mind to." She pointed at the radiant Nia once more. "And you will become her." She then pointed at herself. "And not I."

"Thank you so much for informing me of all this, I really appreciate it!"

"It's my pleasure, Nia. Also, listen to Dad. Your name means purpose and Mom blessed you with that name because your purpose is to have a growth mindset through taking control of your spiritual, mental and physical phases. I know hear Dad's talk as a little interesting at times, but it's also easy to dust him off." They both took a moment to laugh as they recollected their same memories of dismissing their father's communicative efforts.

"But...and this is a big but," she began. "You need to take what he's doing currently and take it to the next level for the legacy of the familial line. Remember mother. Remember Simba. Remember father. Get all the knowledge and wisdom you can get from him now, because everyone has a deadline."

Tears instantly welled up in Nia's eyes as her heart raced at a shocking pace, triggering her anxiety.

"Did Dad die in your time too already?"

Nia's failed future-self sniffed aggressively, and Nia hadn't realized she was crying as well.

"Like I said, I can't spoil the future for you, because that would spoil what's supposed to happen organically, so my mouth is sealed. All I'll say is part of understanding and taking control of the spiritual phase is understanding that we all have a deadline, so have those conversations with him and make the best of the time you have with him while he's here physically. Just do what I said and everything will work out perfectly fine. I can say that much."

"Okay, but I'm just scared, because what if I fail and disappoint everybody that means something to me? Not even that, what if my haters get satisfied from seeing me fail? Or even worse, what if I succeed and those that hate me come after me? That's why I, or we self-sabotage our little successes."

Nia's failed future-self placed her hands on Nia's shoulders intimately.

"Nia, you need to be rewired to know that you don't need to fear failure, because success is pretty much a progressive realization of a worthy ideal."

Nia stared at her confused like she spoke Yoruba.

"Success is a realization of a what? Now you're just talking and not making sense to me! What does all this progressive ideal stuff even mean?"

"Let me explain."

"Go ahead, Kevin Hart."

"Touché. Progressive means it's a process. Failure is just as gradual, so failure and success are very similar. This is why I said you have to view difficult differently and rewire the way your brain functions. I wish I did this. I'm nearly the same as the successful one over there, just slightly different. Failure and success both evoke emotions out of us. Failure evokes a negative one, success evokes a positive one. The way," she stated, pausing briefly as if she were in a deep thought. "I won't say Mrs. so you don't act weird. The way your future successful self thinks is she doesn't view failure as negative, because if she fails 20 times, success might be on the 21st effort. So with that, she looks at her failures as a step before success and the only logical thing she sees fit is looking at them similarly."

"Wow, she's incredible!"

Her hands traveled from Nia's shoulders above her neck as she placed her hands on her cheeks. Nia felt a comfortable warmth.

"You're incredible, Nia."

"Thank you!"

"And one more thing Nia."

"Yeah?"

"Once you master the growth mindset, you will then grasp the golden rule, The Power of Yet."

"The Power...of...Yet?"

Nia's failed future-self now gave off an almost angelic aura as she laughed, despite still looking disheveled.

"You'll know what to do with it when the time comes!"

She smiled, removed her hands from Nia's face and walked away.

4

IT'S A BLESSING
IN DISGUISE!

Nia was awakened by the pure, elegant sound of angels harmoniously performing an orchestral performance. She rose earlier than usual, surprised by the lack of angels in her room. Her room was so dark there wasn't a noticeable difference whether she opened her eyes or made her eyelids meet. With her new-found spiritual awakening, she had evolved spiritually overnight and now viewed this early waking as a divine one, rather than attributing her rise to simply rising up early. This was an early, fortunate stroke of serendipity.

"21-day fast huh? I guess this is the first day. This sounds really outlandish, but I know they're watching me, so I'll do my best I guess." She stretched her body out, letting out a sigh. "*The Four Agreements* never leaves my life it seems."

Her stomach began to growl viciously. She reverted deeply into her negative thoughts once more.

"Should I even go through with this fasting challenge? What is it really going to help me with? I don't want to disappoint Mom and my failed future-self, but I don't know about this stuff. It's just so hard and I can't see myself doing it, realistically. I'm going to feel so weak after it all, and I already feel weak so why bother right?"

She glanced around her room noticing a couple of empty bags of chips. They were scattered along her floor and it nearly killed her. Redirecting her vision towards the surface of her desk, she confused a colorful pen she owned for a piece of candy. Each second seemed longer than the last as she clutched her stomach and the sun hadn't even risen yet. It was already a difficult task for her to pray in the first place as she struggled with her faith often, but she suddenly felt a spiritual surge traveling throughout her body. She found a new element of hope and belief like she had been tired and just consumed her morning coffee as a reset button to desire to accomplish her goal once more.

Nia shook her head and slapped herself on her right cheek gently.

"Stop that 'I can't do it' stuff Nia, that's the negative talk again. That's fixed mindset talk. I gotta rebuke that fixed mindset stuff and be in a growth mindset. I can't let them down so I'm going to do it...I guess."

It was as if her mother was operating through her spiritually. Regardless of that, she was still Nia.

"I believe a little bit, but I know my faith could be stronger, so maybe this is good for me to do. I don't want to do it though." She sighed once again. "I think I'll just let Dad decide and that'll be that, because all this thinking is starting to stress me out and make me even hungrier!"

Retrieving to her father's domain, her eyes were harassed by bright lights. Mr. Akintewe presented her with a confused reaction. It was like he was shocked she was awake, simply because he was conducting business he didn't want anyone else to know about. However, Nia was excessively hungry and sleepy to the point she barely paid attention to his body language and mannerisms.

"What are you doing up so early sweetie? You're ready for your driver's test?"

Nia was now acclimated to the lighting in her father's room and fixed her gaze on him.

"Dad, I'm bored!"

"How can you be bored if you aren't a boring person?"

"Huh?"

"Boredom is a disease honey, remember that. We've been over this. This is why so many people in Notsuoh deviate away from focus and fail. Boredom can distract you and lead you towards a failing path. Boredom is the cousin to failure. I hope you got some sleep too. Remember, adequate relaxation is a part of the grind. Are you ready for your driver's test?"

"I'm over it Dad, it's whatever at this point, but I have a question."

"Yeah?"

"How do you feel about fasting?"

He appeared flabbergasted by her question.

"It's amazing honey! You may not notice, but I fast routinely to give my all to the Creator. It's a token of thanks I'm giving to Him and to practice my own discipline. I fast every Sunday. But this is about you. I know you aren't doing it to lose weight. What are you looking to gain from fasting today?"

Nia grew defensive upon his question.

"Whoa! I didn't say I was fasting *today*, I just asked you how *you* feel about it."

"Well, you're obviously thinking about doing it if you brought it up. You don't exactly just wake up in the middle of the night and start talking about fasting for fun. That's slightly weird, and that's coming from your old man."

"Okay, I'll be honest. I'm trying to fast for 21 days straight."

Her father was taken aback and nearly jumped backward. Nia grew insecure as a result of his reaction.

"What? You don't believe in me, huh?"

He oscillated his hands rapidly in a nervous fashion. "No! No! No! Honey, I believe in you! I just didn't expect that. That's all." He displayed a nervous smirk and clutched the back of his head. "So why do you want to do it?"

"I want to perform a spiritual cleansing of myself, which will lead to a spiritual awakening. I feel like I have a lot of negative energy surrounding me from public speaking and other things, so maybe fasting and working on my relationship with God will help me get over all these issues and any issues I have after these demons are cleansed out of my system."

"Okay I see." He pushed his glasses up using his left index finger and placed it on his chin, his thumb accompanying it, rubbing the scruffy attachment as he analyzed her meticulously. "Before this conversation you used to have problems believing in God and yourself. I don't know why, but I see a new light shining around you. It's like you have a new aura today. And that's a mature self-analysis of yourself. It's *very* important to know yourself."

Nia avoided his eye contact as she felt honored by his compliment, conveniently choosing to look down at the ground.

"Thanks, Dad."

"You're evolving into a young black queen right before my eyes. It's been hard doing this parenting thing on my own, but I'm evolving and starting to finally get the hang of it, just like you and your obstacles. I remember when I had to do your hair when you were younger. Man, that was a nightmare!"

Nia rolled her eyes out of embarrassment.

"Sorry about that sweetie, just reminiscing on the quality time we spent together. Remember, your natural hair is beautiful and don't listen to the naysayers. Anyway, just for your information, I'll tell you how I fast. I pray every three hours and usually start at 6:00 AM and go until 6:00 PM." He glanced over at the clock. "You're up really early and it's a quarter until six. I would advise you to start small, so if you will do it, try today and see how you feel. You can even stop early at 3:00 PM or noon if you want, but it definitely builds discipline." Nia's stomach growled viciously once more. "You've got a couple options. You can choose to not fast and go on about your day and eat, or you can start in 15. Up to you."

"No. I'll do the entire 12 hours Dad."

"That's my disciplined baby girl!" He pinched her cheek lightly. "I could see the determination in your face. I told you to take control of your spirituality, but didn't know it would be this fast, so I'm proud of you! Today is day one then. No pressure though, I believe in you. Besides, you're starting to resemble and give off the energy of your mother. That's a great thing!"

Nia was determined to succeed. There was no going back now. She put it out into the universe to be held accountable. Despite how hungry she felt, she knew that this was a necessary step in order to take control of her life and become the Nia that she needed to be. Not only did she feel more spiritually awakened now, but she was fueled with energy upon the simple act of her father stating he believed in her. She quickly grew more social and decided to take a stab at another question while he routinely sipped on his coffee.

"I have another question."

"Shoot."

"Do you know anything about...The Power of...Yet?"

He choked on his coffee, nearly spitting it out. As a result, he coughed profusely as Nia was unsure if she should attempt to perform a Heimlich maneuver on him. She froze at the fact she was half his size and came to terms with herself it was liquid he was choking on. Standing in front of him awkwardly, she apologized as he performed an animated demonstration. Feeling insecure from his unexpected reaction, she broke her silence as his coughs came to an end.

"What?"

"Nothing, sweetheart. I just think it's a blessing in disguise you brought that to my attention, because I'm currently working on incorporating that exact concept into my speaking topics. I'm thinking about putting out a book addressing that principle as well."

"Oh wow, that's a crazy coincidence! Well, maybe it's a divine occurrence since I had a dream about it."

"That's even more evidence! The fact you brought it up to me is a sign from God I'm headed towards the right path and I'm going to continue to follow the road I've paved so far. I think you just reaffirmed everything I've already thought about." Her father grew emotional out of the blue as he took off his glasses and wiped his eyes, sighing heavily. "I said it's a blessing in disguise you brought it to my attention, because I've been suffering from my own self-doubt a lot lately and not being completely sure if I'm headed in the right path."

Nia was astounded. For her to witness the man she always knew to be so strong placed in a vulnerable position, shocked her. As she laid her eyes on him, she reconsidered how she previously viewed him in a flawless manner. She still admired him for his exemplary guidance, but now viewed him as an imperfect force with more humane qualities. She assumed this situation to be a divine intervention from God as he would say.

"I'm sorry to hear you felt like that." Nia mirrored his emotions as her glasses began to fog up. "Daddy, you guide me when I'm feeling down, but who do you go to when you're feeling down?"

He didn't want to appear vulnerable in front of Nia, because he remembered he was a role model for her. He laughed and sniffed aggressively, either from the morning cold, poignant tears falling, or a combination of both.

"My baby girl is a thinker huh?" He sniffed once more and placed his glasses back on his face and grabbed Nia's shoulders, squatting down to her height. "That's a great question, but your Dad isn't perfect so I won't lie to you and I'll be honest and say I don't go to anyone, but God."

"Why don't you communicate with humans though?"

"That's a great point though. I do help a lot of people and it can be taxing at times." He placed a finger on his chin, stroking his beard and pondered her question. "I think it's important I should be aware of helping myself too. Maybe God wants me to communicate with others as well. Interesting. I'll have to pay more attention to that." He placed his index finger on the tip of Nia's nose. "Thanks baby!"

Nia grew offended.

"Hey! I'm not a baby anymore Dad!"

She chased him around the island counter for a bit while he evaded her gracefully. They slowed down quickly after making one lap. Nia was extremely tired, breathing aggressively. Her father appeared confused as he came to a halt. He placed his hand out as if he was reaching for something, imitating a sign to stop while wearing a stern face of authority.

"I'm just going to let you off the hook and say you're super tired since you didn't eat today, but we need to discuss exercise later. That's a topic for another day though and it's very important to be in tune with yourself."

"Okay Dad."

"More importantly, how far on applying those principles from the Mentor and CEO book?"

Nia paused briefly and froze as if she didn't hear him.

"Huh?"

Her father noticeably got impatient.

"Am I speaking a new language?" He noticed her fearful reaction and his energy became less tense, his voice softening. "It's okay if you didn't, I just want the truth from you. Don't lie to me. You know how I feel about being lied to. That's one of the most disrespectful things you can do to me. So I'm going to ask you again, how far did you get on applying the principles?"

Nia stared at him shockingly as she absorbed each and every word he spewed.

"Remember, there are three types of friends you should have, and I told you mentor and peer were a couple. The last one I didn't mention. I also told you to identify a peer on the same journey as you. Did you at least do that Nia?"

Nia stared at the ground as if the answer was clearly written down there.

"No, I didn't start. I was scared to talk to my classmates and I was mad, because I did terrible on my test." Nia's energy shifted abruptly as she realized she didn't mean to discuss her shortcomings from her test. "Oh! Never mind."

"It's okay. It's actually good you didn't start. Believe it or not, I view it as a blessing in disguise."

Nia wore a confused mask.

"Hear me out. This is an opportunity for me to help you learn how to move forward and redefine how you view failure so you aren't afraid to make that leap."

"Okay Dad."

"Wait! Did you at least finish the book? What's the third type of friend you should have?"

"I didn't finish it, but I did start!" Nia replied, confessing the truth.

"Okay, I think you should move on with reading *Think and Grow Rich* by Napoleon Hill *after* you finish *Mentor: The Kid & The CEO* and when you read that, the principles you find in Napoleon's Hill book should inspire your execution of the principles within the Mentor and CEO and so on. I should have probably started you off with *Think and Grow Rich* to be honest, that's my bad."

"It's okay Dad."

He rummaged through his bag of goods and pulled out an ancient looking version of *Think and Grow Rich,* dusting off dust particles it had accumulated over time. He got ready to hand her the book as she still wore a confused look on her face. He now mirrored her expression, clutching the book tightly in his hand.

"What happened?"

"Dad, I actually have a confession."

"You lied to me? Confess!"

"Well, not exactly. I just didn't fully state some information."

"I'm all ears."

"You were saying that you'll help me fix my view for my fear of failure."

"Yeah?"

"I...I actually have a fear of success."

"Fear of...success?" He folded his arms comfortably. "Elaborate ma'am. I'm going to have to digest this one."

"Well, I don't know if it's just been a spiritual awakening for me to know this about myself, but I recently noticed that I like to self-sabotage my successes, because I fear succeeding more than failing."

"That's tough."

"Yeah. And I'm scared of success, because it's like when I succeed at something, if that ever happens, I don't know who will be for me and who will be against me. And also, I have to keep going once I do it. It's a lot of pressure. Whenever I'm close to being successful, my natural instinct is to mess it up so I don't experience that feeling of pressure."

"That's deep."

"Does that make any sense?"

"Yeah it does. And when you say that, that reminds me about another book I got on my mind for you to read, but we'll revisit that chapter later." He grinned, exposing a blinding set of pearly white teeth. "You really know yourself now! Is that the effect of the fasting already on day one? Wow!"

"Dad, stop."

"Sorry." He pointed to the book he held tightly. "You're going to love this book though! Napoleon Hill is the GOAT!"

Nia was taken aback, moving her head back animatedly, amused.

"Dad, your old generation doesn't know anything about the GOAT. You guys aren't hip!"

"Your old man isn't that old! I lived in the era of watching Michael Jordan play young lady! We invented that term. Y'all youngins came up and snatched it like y'all did something new. Get out of here!"

He loosened his grip and handed her the book. As the book graced her hands, she immediately felt a surge of knowledge running through her veins aggressively upon simply holding it. Tracing her fingertips along the book's surface, she felt spiritually empowered. Thinking about the fact she didn't follow through with what he instructed her to do, she realized some things were indeed a blessing in disguise. Had she listened to him initially, she wouldn't have been able to share this unique experience with him in the moment it occurred and may have never came across the book when she needed it.

"Sweetie, I have my own confession as well. I hope you still love me."

Nia's heart dropped mercilessly.

"W-what happened Dad?"

"You know how I said I struggled with the father stuff early on since I did it on my own? Handling your hair and dealing with periods and all that?"

"Yes?"

"When I figured out we were having you, I actually wanted a son."

Nia's heart dropped. Her voice trembled as she stammered to talk.

"O-o-okay."

"Yeah." He stared up towards the ceiling. "The entire time I envisioned myself having a son and playing basketball with him and not dealing with all the conditions that came with having a daughter."

"Okay. So do you regret having me?"

Her father's heart dropped with hers, as he glanced at the ground.

"Of course not sweetie."

He picked his head up and fixed his gaze on her staring into the deepest abyss of her soul.

"Never that!"

"Why not?"

"I was presented with a wake-up call when you came to the world, because I had to learn and adjust very quickly. I had to change my mindset and grow from a fixed one. It was a lot dealing with you, but you showed me how to love effectively. You made me learn a lot about myself because of those experiences and tiresome nights and I can confidently say that having you in my life now is a blessing. Your life is *my* blessing in disguise."

Nia felt slightly better. That was a good enough answer for her. "Okay Dad, I love you again." She hugged him tightly.

"It's still pretty early sweetie." He yawned as he began to return back to his room. "Your driving test isn't for a couple hours. I'm going to take a nap and then we can head over."

"Sounds good to me."

It was just her and the book standing in the kitchen. She curled the book with both hands like she was performing a bicep curl and thought to herself how powerful she felt. She began getting an itch to start the book. On the fence about it for a bit, she quickly came to an agreement with herself that she would listen to her father and start the book after finishing *Mentor: The Kid & The CEO.*

She now knew with certainty she would fast for 21 days. This day would be the first day of her 21-day adventure. She glanced over at the clock in the kitchen and noticed it was after six.

"Shoot! I should pray first, and then I'll read."

Nia returned to her room and prayed. For what seemed like an eternity to her, she prayed to her satisfaction, making sure she addressed combating the trials and tribulations of each and every person she cared about. This was a very small list, but she got the job done. Following the prayer, she felt a content cleanse throughout her spirit, despite feeling miserable about being hungry in her physical form. However, the good outweighed the bad in this scenario, so all was well with her as far as she was concerned.

She quickly finished *Mentor: The Kid & The CEO* and found it to be a touching story. Figuring out the third type of companion she should have, she wondered why her father placed emphasis on it.

"So there's mentor, peer and the part Dad was talking about me reading was *mentee*? He was making a fuss over some *mentee*? What's that about?"

She closed the book and threw it to the side, glancing over at *Think and Grow Rich* with excitement. Eyes strained from reading, she opened the book of knowledge out of curiosity and began speed reading through it. It was like time ceased as she kept flipping the pages, one after the other. She read about the importance of having a definitive purpose and found a personal alignment with the meaning of her name. The book now possessed a closer connection with her, because she knew that her parents were always discussing that *Think and Grow Rich* book, according to her father.

She grew emotional as she read the book. She felt a deep connection with Napoleon Hill using his palette to paint the story of her life's struggles, poignant tears meandering down her face onto the pages. Feelings of regret for discovering the book later than she desired lingered in her mind. As she read Hill's stance on faith, her eyes fogged up to the point she couldn't see the pages clearly while the message was crystal clear, one word after the other.

She grew more spiritually aware of the fact she was visited in her dream purposefully, and the timing of the request for her to begin her 21-day fasting journey was becoming clearer by the second. She was consciously aware and reminded of Notsuoh's nature, residents having the choice to focus or fail. She decided with certainty she would complete the 21-day fast to follow the path of focus. More spiritually conscious than before as a result of a few experiences and one deep prayer, she had the mental capacity to recognize this was truly a blessing in disguise.

Her father walked in her room whilst wiping his eyes. He appeared lost as a result of waking up from his slumber. After dusting off a couple eye boogers and seeing clearly, he grew worried, scrunching his face when he laid eyes on Nia.

"You alright sweetie?"

Nia set the book down, the front cover meeting the bed's surface. She fixed her gaze on him, crying profusely. He looked down on her bed and flipped the book over and read the front cover as his heart galloped.

"Aww sweetie, you began the book already. Come on over here."

He stretched his arms out to her and they embraced one another, both understanding the potency of the emotional tie the book held on their family.

"This book will change your life." He loosened his grip on her fragile body. He analyzed her facial expression, observing her persistent tears streamlining down her face excessively. He attempted to lighten the mood. "I told you Napoleon Hill is the GOAT!"

"Yeah…"

He caressed her hair delicately, wiping the tears off her face.

"See this?"

He brought his fingers to her attention.

"Yeah?"

"These tears are all the demons of fear, fear of success and failure, and a fixed mindset spirit all transcending into a blessing. A growth mindset."

She felt calmer, as if she felt the effect of the demons being removed from her body instantly.

"You promise, Dad?"

"Yes."

He glanced over where *Mentor: The Kid & The CEO* lay. He now wore an expression informing her he had on his thinking cap.

"So if you've been reading *Think and Grow Rich* that means you finished the mentor book already. What are the three types of friends you should have?"

Nia sniffed and cleared her throat as she prepared her response.

"Yes sir. I finished it, and the three types of friends are mentors, peers, and… mentees?"

"Yes!" He wore an expression as if he had been finally freed from a spiritual battle. "Finally! Thank you for listening. You know why I told you to read that and didn't tell you what the answer was?"

"Why?"

"The answer was in the book. Mentees. If you have a mentee that means you're a mentor leading someone. If you can't follow simple instructions from *your* mentor, scanning words on a page, then you don't deserve to be leading anyone. I say that, because when you didn't listen you still had traits you needed to fix within yourself, so who are you to lead someone if you can't lead yourself?"

"You swear you're Yoda or something with all these tests!"

"It's only helping you." He chuckled upon digesting her remark. "But who are you and who am I?"

"I'm Nia Akintewe, and you're my father who loves me."

"What do you deserve?"

"I deserve all the love in the world!"

"What are the three pillars for financial freedom to get rid of your student loan debt or overcome anything you encounter?"

"Believe. Plan. Execute."

"And why is gratitude so important?"

"You can't be great without being grateful, it's in the word if you reverse the letters."

"Great! Go get ready and let's go to your driving test."

She sighed heavily.

"Okay."

They made their way over to the Department of Motor Vehicles. As they arrived it hit her. Nia's heart beat rapidly upon entering the same building that had been causing her trauma for quite some time. Upon her spiritual awakening, she believed today would be different, because she now felt like she had a growth mindset and cried her demons out of her like her father suggested.

In what seemed like a blink of an eye, she began hyperventilating in the corner standing up taking her test. Her legs were buckling for strength as her hands were shaking noticeably as if she had Parkinson's disease. She grew paranoid about her answers to the point she began whispering the basics to herself to ensure her brain was functioning correctly.

"Okay Nia. Red means stop. Green means go. Red means gre— I mean stop! Red means stop."

In what was a well-ventilated air conditioned area, she started to feel a hot flash and began perspiring heavily. She felt distracted, losing her focus as she attempted to find similarities from the last driving test she failed. This was her last resorted effort to maintain her grip at success, nearly falling to shambles by the second. When she found none and realized she possessed a completely revised, new test, she began to go into panic mode. Her attempt at processing her thoughts in a robotic manner were rejected when she glanced up at the corner of the test, reading a new version name. Not only that, much time had elapsed since she last took the test so new rules had been implemented and changed accordingly.

"Dang it!"

She slammed her fist on the table as she realized what had occurred.

A couple of test takers peeked in her direction, observing the commotion. She awkwardly glanced at them and went back to staring at her paper as if she was in deep thought. She slowly looked back at them and noticed they had returned back to taking their respective tests. She whispered to herself once more.

"Yeah that's right. You better go back to taking your test. You wanna waste your time and stare at me? Don't worry about me!"

Nia took a deep breath and proceeded to find her focus and prevent failure. With her back against the wall, she read questions she didn't immediately know the answer to as she twiddled her pencil in her hand nervously. The pencil suddenly left her grip, dropping to the ground. When it met the ground, it let off a loud ring to her ears, louder than the sound it should have made. Scrambling for it on the ground as it rolled away from her arm's reach, she bumped into an individual taking a test; he was one of the individuals that stared at her when she abused the table's surface. His face grew red and he glared at her unforgivingly.

"I'm sorry about that."

He maintained his furious gaze on her and wiped his arm as if she had transmitted an illness onto him. Going back to taking his test, he revealed his profile with noticeably red inflamed ears.

Rolling her eyes, she continued following the path of her pencil. "I said I was sorry," she whispered to herself, shaking her head.

Nia picked up her pencil, receiving new-found courage to finish the test out of thin air. Although she was enduring a mental struggle between finishing it and not finishing it, she overcame that battle by first believing in herself. Her spiritual acumen was evolving by the second. She finished the test and lined up to hear the verdict, waiting for a few gruesome minutes before it was her turn to experience heart palpitations.

The woman behind the desk making or breaking people's days was a middle-aged woman. She sported ginger colored hair in two buns, with grey strands running through the crevice of her scalp, stress and age being the culprit. She had pale, wrinkly skin and barely visible lips; she wore red lipstick, but her lips were still noticeably chapped at the same time. It didn't take a rocket scientist to notice she was overweight, despite the fact she sat down and one could only view the top half of her body.

Nia instantly noticed her energy was uncanny. She conducted herself in a manner where her energy expressed she didn't want to be there. Raising her heels and placing weight emphasis on the balls of her feet, Nia attempted to hand the woman her test, and the woman nearly snatched it out of her hand aggressively.

"I would be mad if I worked at the DMV too," Nia whispered to herself.

She read the name tag on the woman: Sarah.

"I would be mad too...Sarah."

Sarah leaned towards Nia, revealing a mole on her left cheek with hairs protruding out in various directions.

"What was that?"

"Nothing," Nia responded with a nervous chuckle. "Just talking to myself."

Sarah wore thick brown glasses that hung from her nose. She stared at Nia eerily, fixing her focus back on preparing to grade the exam. She wondered how Sarah was able to see for the simple fact her glasses were worn so low.

Nia glanced over at her father. Right on time, his eyes met hers and he smiled vibrantly in her direction, giving her a nod of acknowledgment. His legs were crossed while he wore his fancy attire, exuding off the characteristics of a carefree black man. He wore a red sports coat and golden framed glasses, sticking out like a sore thumb amongst the rest of the crowd dressed in mundane attire. He always warned her to stay ready and sharp when it came to the way one dressed because you never knew who you would encounter at a moment's notice. She glanced down at herself and witnessed the same yellow hoodie she always wore, and proceeded to fix her gaze back on Sarah.

Sarah retrieved the answer bank from behind her chair. Licking her index and middle fingers simultaneously, she flipped carelessly through the pages until finding the answer bank she sought. She was old fashioned. She squinted as she scanned the answers and Nia's responses, alerting Nia she suffered from farsightedness. Nia began hyperventilating once more as she witnessed Sarah glance over the first few answers; she didn't mark anything yet.

All of a sudden, two consecutive marks was enough to make Nia ready to pass out momentarily. She felt a metallic taste in the back of her throat and started to feel like she would vomit and pass out simultaneously. Her heart was dropping. She glanced away immediately for the remainder of the grading for the sake of her health. Following the sound of a number of sporadic hand gestures, she heard Sarah clear her throat.

"Excuse me! Take it. Here you go!"

Heart pacing and fingers trembling, Nia retrieved the test and there lied the verdict illustrated in capital letters on the paper.

FAIL.

Upon reading the letters illustrated emphatically, the formation of Nia's tears nearly commenced. However, there was a weird feeling surrounding the feelings of disappointment and sadness. She wasn't as disappointed the first few times and couldn't pinpoint why. She wasn't sure if she was getting acclimated to failing, or if she encountered another blessing in disguise, but she knew deep in her soul this wasn't the end of the world despite the fact she didn't feel content. Whether her slight resilience may have been also attributed to her newfound spiritual awareness, she didn't know. Nonetheless, she did fail again and felt a degree of disappointment in herself.

Wiping away the initial tears and making her best effort to keep herself composed, she began making her way towards her father with the test in hand, and he immediately understood the verdict from a mile away. They exited the building and walked towards the car silently. Words weren't needed for the mutual understanding Nia didn't care for communication. She walked at a faster pace than her father, nearly leaving him in the dust.

"Nia," he began, letting out a sigh as they approached the car. "I'm not even going to put a disclaimer with this, but you should be appreciative of this experience, because like I told you, failure is a state of mind. This is an opportunity to go back to your plan. Remember I said you have to believe, plan and then execute?"

Nia nodded her head nonchalantly without looking at him, frustrated at his motivational spiels.

"This is an opportunity for you go back to the second step of planning and refine it, so in this case, this is more practice, because this failure could potentially save your life down the line, so it's a blessing in disguise. When you fail to plan, you plan to fail. You understand me?"

"Yes, I understand," she replied genuinely, nodding her head.

"Good sweetie. Let's say you don't get accepted into UCLA," he began, as her heart raced rapidly. "It's a blessing in disguise *because* from that 'failure' there's a lesson to be learned and you should look at it as God redirecting you. Another way to put it is you're being 'divinely redirected' so *essentially* you have to view failure differently. Don't say you were rejected, you were divinely redirected. Don't say you were rejected, you were divinely redirected!"

Nia grew conscious of the fact her failed future-self instructed her to be intentional about listening to her father's rambling.

"Okay I get you. You're right Dad."

She walked over to the passenger seat of the car, opened her door and they began their journey home.

On the way home, they were silent for nearly half the duration of the trip and he broke the silence.

"So are you hungry?" he inquired, glancing at her as they approached a red light.

"No, I'm fasting Dad. You should know this already," she replied, calmly crossing her arms.

"Oh! My bad sweetie, I forgot, but that's great!"

"Yeah, so now I gotta go home and thank the Lord, because it's a blessing in disguise right?"

He glanced at her once more happily.

"Yeah sweetie you got it!" he replied ecstatically.

"It ain't no stupid blessing!" Nia grew furious he failed to pick up on her sarcasm. "I was being sarcastic. This is so stupid and I don't know why I keep failing that stupid test. I'm never going to drive. Driving is dumb anyway if you ask me." Her father remained silent to give her an avenue to vent. Nia sighed. "I guess I'll thank God for the experience. I'm just frustrated even if it's somehow some kind of blessing. It's hard looking at my mishaps as some undercover blessing."

Her father nodded his head. "That's understandable, and that's why I'm not refuting anything you're saying. You have a right to be upset, but don't let that control your life. Use that feeling as fuel to move forward and make adjustments. Believe. Plan. Execute." He tapped her shoulder. "And Nia, execute aggressively."

They pulled up to the driveway, arriving home. She noticed her father scrunching his face in the manner that she often did and thought to herself how similar the two of them were. She wondered what he was thinking about.

"Let me see the exam. I want to see something."

She reached into the pouch of her hoodie and handed it to him. Growing tired of the interaction surrounding the test, she stepped out of the car quickly and made her way inside to get away from the situation and perform her next prayer. As she made her way to the front door, she glanced back at him and noticed him in the car staring at the paper meticulously.

"This old man is looking at the paper looking dumb like he knows what's going on," Nia began, chuckling. "The driving rules probably changed since the last time he took it anyway."

Nia made her way inside. She was amused at how her father's focus. She returned to her room to sing praises and read her Bible before her prayer. She successfully completed the prayer and felt even more spiritually awakened. She even felt ready to study and give the test another shot in a couple weeks.

There was something so deep and powerful about the art of prayer and taking the time out of the day to communicate with the Heavenly Father. She didn't know why it had such a heavy impact on her, but she wanted to continue chasing that blissful feeling and questioned why she hadn't been fasting her entire life. She made a mental note to inform her future mentee about fasting.

Nia returned to the living room and her father was still not inside. She began growing angry because it was as if he subconsciously made the test a lingering thought for her. This feeling of feeling attacked by her father was starting to get on her last nerves.

Returning back outside to meet him, she prepared hypothetical conversations that included her being dominant over him in conversation.

"I'm gonna be like 'Dad! What did I tell you about that damn test? Enough is enough! Stop looking at it!' And he's gonna be like 'Sorry sweetie, it won't happen again' and that's how it'll go!"

Nia paced back and forth before meeting her father as she hyped herself up. She swore her orchestrated dialogue with herself was how the conversation with her father would transpire. Meeting her father, she observed him in the same position as if he never moved a centimeter. She began her attempt to simulate what she had planned, but something else came out.

"Uh Dad, are you uh, still looking at my...test?"

"Nia sweetie, you actually passed," he replied, calmly ignoring her.

Nia wore a confused look.

"Um, what do you mean? I passed the door to get inside the house or what do you mean, because I know I didn't pass the *test*?"

"I mean you passed your exam," he stated nonchalantly. He signaled a hand motion for her to enter the passenger side. "Get in the car, we're going to drive back *right now*!"

Nia placed her little self in the car at his command, alarmingly confused. She wondered how she passed if she missed enough questions to fail the exam.

"Nia listen here. It's really a blessing in disguise that you didn't rip up the test this time. That composure was key. That's what I mean about viewing difficult differently! I thought it was weird that you failed again, so I was just curious as to what you were getting wrong. I looked at your test and she marked answers wrong that you *clearly* got correct." He shrugged his shoulders. "And who knows, maybe you passed the test previous times as well, but we'll never know since you ripped them."

"Whatever Dad," Nia replied slightly embarrassed of her past behavior.

"I told you to view difficult differently to have a growth mindset for success, and you displayed it through your actions beautifully. This is what I mean! I'm proud of you for the growth in not tearing this test. But you've got to trust yourself Nia! Let this be a lesson. Just because someone says you're wrong doesn't necessarily mean you're wrong. You'll have a lot of your peers and even professors questioning your intelligence when you're a Computer Scientist so you better get used to it now. That's all I'm saying."

He floored the gas pedal as they sped at an uncomfortable speed for Nia's mental health. She felt like she was in *Fast and Furious* while hoping her father was correct about the miscalculated test. He quickly noticed she grew uncomfortable with his speed and he slowed down rapidly. Arriving back at the Devil's Palace, her father opened up his door aggressively and instructed her to step out.

Nia noticed an instantaneous shift in his mood, driven from relaxed to angry. She was baffled, because she now felt like he was the one that failed the test instead of her. She hadn't seen him like this in quite some time. Despite her perplexing feeling, she recognized her father valued respecting himself and others, and receiving that respect back. When he felt he was being disrespected, it wasn't a good sign for anyone that crossed his path. She arrived at the thought he felt Sarah intentionally disrespected her through failing her deliberately.

They walked inside once more. Nia followed her father as he walked up to where Sarah was still checking exams, cutting various individuals in the process. Sarah noticed him standing near her as she assisted an elderly black woman.

"Sir, you can't come up right now. There are a lot of people waiting in line. You'll have to go to the back of the line and hold up for—"

"Ain't no hold up!" He glanced over at the elderly black woman being assisted. "My apologies ma'am," he stated calmly. "Can I handle something really quick?" She nodded her head and took a step back for him to intervene and deal with Sarah accordingly.

"You failed my daughter for what reason?"

"She failed the exam."

"I looked at the answers she put and graded it myself and she didn't fail, let me see the version key you used."

"No! There are a lot of customers waiting. Go ahead and move along!"

"Bring...it...out!"

"No!"

As they played tug of war verbally with one another, slinging negative words at one another, they sparked a commotion for all to see. She aggressively retrieved the answer key to hasten their departure. She slammed the book on the surface in the process.

"And who decided to urinate in your cereal this morning ma'am?"

"Excuse me? Are you threatening me?"

"No one is threatening you. You're giving off an unnecessary attitude when we want to confirm if she passed. You've threatened my daughter *if* you failed her on purpose."

"You're not right. I literally graded her test." She scanned the versions. "Okay. This is the one I used. What version did your daughter have?"

"619."

Her father glanced over the divider between them and observed the page read: 916.

"You used version 916 and she had test version 619. Are we claiming dyslexia on this one or you disrespected my daughter?"

"Wow! I didn't know it was the wrong version. That sucks."

Nia's father handed Sarah the exam as Sarah glanced through it and realized Nia passed. She poignantly changed the exam to a passing grade. Inscribing "pass" in all lower case letters, she handed the test back to Mr. Akintewe aggressively, without making eye contact with either of them. Sarah grew red knowing that she had just been made a fool of in front of everyone. They retrieved back to the car with a victory.

As they drove home, Nia reflected on the situation as her father cued Tobe Nwigwe's "I'm Dope" on the car's sound system. He's dope. Her father's dope. She's dope. She was in awe of how it all transpired. She was occupied pondering about the situation the entire duration of the journey home, and failed to process her thoughts and articulate it verbally. She reclaimed her thoughts as they arrived home. She decided to break her silence with her father as they stepped out of the car.

"I think that situation taught me something."

"What did it teach you sweetie?"

Nia realized he returned to his mellow self.

"If that situation didn't humble me by showing me what *could* actually be, with me failing the exam, I wouldn't be motivated to be successful in other avenues in my life. Seeing what *can* potentially happen puts things into perspective. Also, I wouldn't be where I'm supposed to be. I think I'm on the right path and this spiritual journey is helping me. I'm not even near the 21st day of my fast, so I can only imagine how much more I'll grow in the process!"

"That's what I'm telling you about the concept of a blessing in disguise," he replied playfully. "One more thing, Nia."

"Yeah."

"An idle hand is an instrument for the Devil."

"What does that mean?"

"Boredom is a disease. If you're sitting around bored not using your hands, they're idle and free for devilish manipulation to occur. The Devil will use your hands if they aren't occupied. Use your hands to focus and pray, or fail."

Nia walked inside her house determined to continue her fasting journey. This was indeed what he said it was: a blessing in disguise.

SPIRITUAL EXERCISES

WHAT'S YOUR RELATIONSHIP WITH MONEY?

In the spiritual phase, Nia recalls the death of her brother Simba. His death is attributed to the fact that he failed to establish a relationship with money. It's important to define your relationship with money in order to take control of money rather than allowing it to take control of you. When you establish this relationship and take control, you're granted the opportunity to rid yourself of any debt you accrue.

The spiritual phase is controlled when you apply the power of belief from within. *Writing information is important because humans forget, while written down information doesn't. Take out a piece of paper and/or write below.*

What's your relationship with money? *Whether you wrote it down below or on a separate piece of paper, take out an additional piece of paper and copy your answer onto the new sheet. Fold this sheet of paper and carry it with you until you finish this book.* ***This is key!*** *Pray daily that you are granted the knowledge and wisdom to establish this relationship within your spirit.*

WHAT'S YOUR AFFIRMATION?

Nia and her father participate in a routine affirming Nia's self-worth. Affirmations are pivotal for the development of one's confidence and self-worth. This is an important activity to implement in your regimen as it pertains to taking control of your life or having that extra boost of confidence towards paying off your debts. Affirmations are a new element of hope and belief like the morning coffee many need as a reset button for motivation towards accomplishing their goals. Think about a way to affirm yourself.

Who are you? Who loves you? Do you love yourself? When will you get rid of your student loans? What do you deserve? What do you desire? Why is gratitude important? Write it down.

Now take out an additional piece of paper and copy your affirmation onto the new sheet. Return back to this page and repeat your affirmation daily (e.g. a routine affirming the fact that you'll pay off your student loan balance or desire to achieve anything in the universe) until you finish this book. Repeat your affirmation on the piece of paper daily until you reach the end of this book. Repetition is required!

The spiritual phase is controlled when you apply the power of belief from within. *Pray daily that you are granted the knowledge and wisdom to fix your affirmations within your spirit.*

MAXIMIZE YOUR INSECURITIES!

Nia has many insecurities and discovered how her father dealt with his own. Think about an insecurity you have. **Write it down. Write them down.** *Now write down an actionable step you can use to maximize it in order to use it as advantageous fuel. Take out an additional piece of paper and copy your answer onto the new sheet. Fold this sheet of paper and carry it with you until you finish this book.*

The spiritual phase is controlled when you apply the power of belief from within. *Pray daily that you are granted the knowledge and wisdom to use your insecurities as advantageous fuel.*

_____

_____

_____

_____

_____

_____

_____

_____

_____

_____

_____

_____

_____

_____

_____

_____

_____

_____

_____

_____

To the misguided and undecided mind

Whose trials and tribulations contribute to a lack of control,

This phase is especially for you

As you plan your goal with heart and soul.

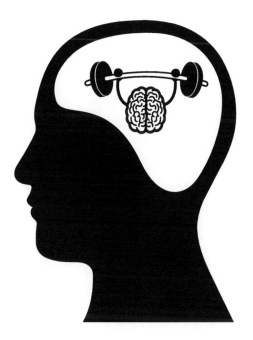

PART II

MENTAL PHASE

5

I GIVE UP

One week went by and it seemed like life was progressively getting better. It was the seventh day of Nia's fasting journey and she had been steady sailing and consistently growing spiritually, performing her daily prayers. It gradually became an easier task to perform due to muscle memory. She rose up from her sleep and realized she was up unusually early. Hearing sporadic movements circulating around the house, she was alerted her father was awake as well.

Nia had been rising up as early as her father upon starting her spiritual journey. Knowing the fact her father would be proud of her for being awake early, she mustered the little bit of strength she had to rise up and make her presence known. Following a few yawns, she stretched her little body as far as it could go along her bed and jumped up off her bed.

"Thank God it's—"

FA-THUD!

She made a loud sound with her fall, catapulting on the floor's wooden surface. She simultaneously collided with her dresser, banging her head in the process. This was an unexpected way to make her presence known to her father. Rising up slowly, she was slightly dizzy, but certainly wide awake now.

"Ouch. This would happen to me. Well, Dad probably knows I'm up now anyway so no use going out there to embarrass myself." Yawning once more, she caressed the top of her head profusely. "Well, it's day seven. I guess this isn't so bad anymore though."

Despite nearly perfecting it as a routine, fasting for her was now more of a mental battle than anything. Even though fatigue plagued her mind day in and day out, she was persevering as best as she could. Realizing she had taken control of the spiritual aspect of the challenge, she knew the next phase of her development on her journey depended on focusing on the mental battles thrown at her.

With a few pages left to savor, Nia finished reading *Think and Grow Rich*. She felt a spiritual surge travel throughout her entire body like she had been set free from the tight grasp of a demon manipulating her idle hands. It was the same feeling as when her hands first met the book's surface, tracing the lines on the cover with her fingers. However, this time she felt an unfamiliar feeling, a mentally inducing feeling. She had a sudden itch to plan out her life. She decided to visit YouTube to live her life vicariously through content creators.

As soon as her finger stroked the 'y' key, YouTube was immediately suggested and she pounded 'enter' with hasteful aggression. Nia witnessed UCLA related videos on her screen based on her watch history, and realized how she prioritized most of her time. As she began typing the letter "c" for measure, many college related suggestions appeared, and she pressed backspace, proceeding to click on a random UCLA vlog.

As the video loaded, she opened up an additional tab to focus on her rebuttal personal statement about why she deserved admission into UCLA. Over the course of the week, she had completed applications for various other schools she initially was rejected from, heeding her father's words of fostering an abundance mindset. She had made much progress over the course of starting her fasting journey and wanted to continue to build upon her foundation.

"It's all mental." Nia put her hand on her mouth in shock as the words blurted out of her mouth fluidly. "Where did those words come from? Was that someone talking through me spiritually or me?"

Nia exuded zero effort toward comprehending this unexpected occurrence and began writing. As she began writing, her ideas seemed to flow effortlessly; she was no longer trapped in a mental cage experiencing a writer's block. She persisted typing swiftly and aggressively in her attempt to collect all her thoughts on paper like it was on the tip of her brain, waiting to fall off into the dark abyss of nothingness.

She typed nearly for an hour, failing to realize the video in the other tab was a playlist of different vlogs. She took a brief break to visit the tab. As she went back to the tab, she witnessed a suggested video on the side titled: What They Don't Tell You About College.

"That seems interesting."

As the person in the vlog was about to close out their video and request the audience to subscribe to their channel, Nia quickly clicked on the video link on the side that initially captured her attention. She found the title interesting, but it wasn't interesting enough to get her away from her aggressive writing while her ideas were alive and well. As the video loaded, she returned back to her application tab where she was making progress on her personal statement. Upon clicking back, she realized she was shut out of the application website.

Her heart raced aggressively. "No!" She began shaking. "No, this can't be."

She used her fidgeting fingers to reopen the tab in hope her progress wasn't meaningless. As the page loaded to reveal the verdict, her blood pressure quickly rose. When it finally loaded she realized her progress was erased, like she never opened the application an hour prior. After working tirelessly and diligently for nearly an hour, she had nothing to show for it. Tears forming and blurred vision occurring, she removed her glasses and tossed them on top of her bed as she followed with a barrage of closed fist punches directed at the bed's surface.

She beat her bed mercilessly as if it stole something. Falling into victim mode, she recollected the series of unfortunate events that led up to this unforeseeable moment. She launched herself around her room like a rag doll into banging her head, and now she had conducted a meaningless hour. The fact she made just as much progress as being stagnant for the past hour killed her. Like a thief in the night, the video on the other tab rose up in volume with adequate inflection to grab her attention instantly.

"*College teaches you how to be an employee,*" the video began.

She clicked back to the YouTube tab and witnessed a man in front of a camera informing her of a new phenomenon she was unfamiliar with. Observing him, she saw an average looking Asian man on the surface, but knew in her mind he possessed a unique aura about him. Something about the way he carried himself made her want to digest what he had to say next.

"It's a poverty mindset," he continued. Nia was hooked to his initial words and no longer worried about her lost pages. She leaned into the screen waiting for what he was going to say next. *"It's a poverty mindset to depend on another person to pay you every two weeks when you can become your own boss, but—"*

Nia quickly paused the video and closed her laptop shut, initiating a banging sound. Upon that action, she remembered she was upset about her lost effort and rushed out of her room and headed downstairs to speak to her father. She was an expert at running away from the source of her problems.

"I give up," she stated to herself.

She made sure she maintained an angry demeanor about her so she would receive his attention with minimal effort. Nia was upset about what had happened to her, but she was more so curious to discuss the content of the video to receive clarity of her father's opinion about college.

Making her way downstairs towards the kitchen, she noticed her father calmly reading a newspaper. She stood still in his presence and he didn't budge. It killed her when he didn't give her the attention she desired at a moment's notice. Glancing up from his newspaper, he slightly pushed his glasses up with his left hand and cleared his throat as he scanned her.

"I heard a pretty big fall up there sweetie. You alright?"

He immediately glanced back at his newspaper and flipped the page.

Nia grew offended.

"So you heard me and you didn't even come and see how I was feeling?"

"Well I mean—"

"No excuses Dad!"

"So that's what we're doing now?"

Nia paused and relaxed her body language; she displayed an amusing shift from a lion demanding its respect from an inferior opponent to a shy girl in a public setting.

"Dad. I give up."

Picking up on her shift in energy, Mr. Akintewe glanced back at her once more. He stared at her attentively. He placed his newspaper on the table and realized it was time for him to give her the attention she desired.

"What do you mean sweetie? What did I tell you about using that kind of language?"

"I don't feel like I'm worthy to exist. I don't feel like being here. I just give up."

"Wait! Wait! What about all the fasting you've been doing? You've been good over the past week?"

"Well yeah, but I don't know. I guess it gets good and then it gets worse, and the worst. I give up."

"No, you don't." He placed his right hand on his scruffy chin. "Tell me Nia," he instructed.

Her eyes were fixed on him. She always recognized when he called her by her name he was ready to participate in a serious conversation.

"Anything on your mind you wanna share?"

Nia took a deep breath as if she had rehearsed this exact moment for years and was ready to recite her performance.

"I fell when I woke up like some weird person to start it all off. And then I was typing my application to try and go to UCLA. I was typing forever and then basically I clicked on YouTube in a different tab and then when I went back to keep typing, all my freakin' words were gone!"

Maintaining his composure, he calmly attempted to extinguish the heat of the situation by avoiding an overreaction. He nodded his head as he waited for her to expose the remainder of her frustration.

"And then, I was watching some video that I randomly clicked on, because it sounded interesting and the title was something about what they don't tell you about college or something like that."

"That's cool," her father interjected, nodding sporadically.

"Then when I was listening to the video, it was some entrepreneur guy talking about how college teaches you to be an employee and have a poor person's mindset. That made me reconsider everything I'm doing and if what I'm doing is really how it's supposed to be. Like, am I on the right path? Maybe I should open my own Computer Science business for marginalized women? Am I meeting the right people? Am I even—"

"Hey," her father began, welcoming her with a warm embrace. "Just try to relax, you're doing perfectly fine. And I like the idea of opening up your own Computer Science space for marginalized women. It's important to own. When you don't have student loan debt, you own your dollars."

"Okay thanks Dad, but I wanted your opinion on the video. College. Is it really that necessary? Is college a waste of time? And I want the *honest* answer!"

Her father smirked and pushed himself back slightly, as if he was offended.

"I could *only* give you the honest answer. Come on, you should know me by now."

"Okay," Nia began, snapping her fingers. "Chop! Chop! Let's hear it then!"

"Listen baby," he began as he wore a look to convey he was about to disappoint her.

"I'm listening."

"College *is* important. It's important to be educated, but try to remember you have to focus on building connections through networking in the process. *That's* the part most people don't place a priority on. I forgot to even tell you to focus on networking, so I'm glad we're revisiting this topic. College is important, education is the most important. College is simply a convenient means and one of the ways to acquire education."

"Okay, I'm listening," Nia replied attentively.

"Networking is the most important part of the equation, in my opinion, so make the best of your situation while you're there. I forgot to tell you that in our last conversation about college. I think it was a blessing in disguise that you stumbled upon that video to be quite honest. Speaking of networking, I want you to get involved with the National Society of Black Engineers when you're majoring in Computer Science. It's a national organization for engineers referred to as NSBE, and it gave me countless opportunities towards success when I was a Computer Science major."

"Hmm," she replied with her finger on her chin as she fell in a deep thought. "Okay

Daddy."

Still not convinced, Nia returned to her room without uttering another word. Sitting on her bed, she aimlessly wondered what to do with her life. She opened her laptop once more and proceeded with the idea to finish the video for guidance.

"I give up," she muttered to herself, falling in a face palm as her laptop loaded up its system.

As the laptop screen welcomed her with a bright interface, she laid her eyes on the video she paused. Feeling discouraged, she moved the cursor to the upper right hand corner slowly as she got ready to exit the tab.

Having a change of heart ignited out of curiosity, she played the video back a few seconds and pressed play.

"College teaches you how to be an employee."

She paused the video once more to collect her thoughts.

"And Dad wants to say that college and networking are important when this guy is telling me not to go to college anymore. *Networking! Networking!* He doesn't know what he's talking about. I might drop out. I might!"

She continued the video.

"It's a poverty mindset to depend on another person to pay you every two weeks when you can become your own boss, but listen to this next part that's very important. It's important to remember college *can* be beneficial if you focus on building those relationships you'll use over time. You *must* network. Let me repeat myself: network!"

Nia paused the video while gasping. It was like the man in the video knew Nia's father and they were both conspiring a prank on her. The man repeated what her father had just told her. It was amusing it took a random individual repeating what her father essentially stated in order for her to credit any validation to her father's statement. A light bulb lit in Nia's head as it finally hit her.

"I need to listen to Dad."

She made a promise with herself to focus on building relationships and found new motivation to reproduce what she once lost on paper.

"With this promise to myself, I'm going to submit my UCLA application in the next week. I have to do it not only for Simba, but for myself!"

She ran downstairs in search for a quick snack, stealthily avoiding interaction with her father. Nia didn't like admitting when she was wrong and would often run away from confessing the other party was correct because that was the most convenient option at her disposal under pressure.

Opening the refrigerator, she felt her father's stare as he flipped through his newspaper. She quickly scanned the contents and noticed an apple. Its bright red, vibrant hue caught her eye. It stuck out from the rest of the items, making it an attractive option. She grabbed it quickly and made her voyage back upstairs. As she began running, she suddenly fell aggressively.

FA-THUD!

"Mmm!" She held in letting out an exaggerated outcry in her attempt to minimize the perceived severity of the fall.

"Honey! You okay?"

"Yes. I'm good Dad." Nia wasn't good. Glancing at her left knee, she witnessed a slight laceration and felt a stinging feeling as the adrenaline had ceased. Redirecting her focus towards her right hand, the apple was still in her possession. "At least this baby's okay."

She kissed the apple and proceeded upstairs with a slight limp.

As she arrived in her room, she set her apple down on top of a piece of Kleenex tissue. Letting out the exaggerated gasp she had been dying to let out, she launched a fist on top of her bed. Picking up the apple, she engraved her teeth in it so deeply the apple rested in between her two front teeth as the seed of knowledge ran through her mind. Ideas were flowing through her mind more fluidly than earlier, as she glanced at the clock in her room.

It was time to be on her way to school. Realizing she had to communicate with her father at some point, she picked up her bag and made her way downstairs, taking bites of her apple in between her steps.

"I'm ready for school, father."

"We're pretty formal this morning huh?" He looked up from his newspaper at her. "An apple a day gives you knowledge today!"

They made their way to the car when Nia suddenly experienced a brain fart upon entering the car. Her ideas for her essay ceased.

"Dad, I don't know why, and I don't know how to explain this—"

"Go ahead, sweetie. Let it all out."

"I don't know how to explain this, but basically before we got in the car, I had a lot of ideas I wanted to put in my essay for the UCLA app, but now it's all lost. And it happened as soon as I stepped foot inside the car."

Her father paused for quite some time. It got to the point she assumed he completely disregarded her concern, as he initiated lane changes and participated in a succession of left and right turns.

"I've been thinking," her father began, alerting her her situation didn't go unnoticed. "And I've noticed that you're a creative. You said your knowledge base of information stopped as soon as you entered the car. When you ate the apple, the ideas were flowing. That's why I said the apple gave you knowledge. But as a creative, and the type of creative you are, your creativity can't be marginalized in a box for the purpose of you being favorably creative."

"What does that mean?"

"Basically look! We're inside a car and it's symbolically a box. When you're outside of this structure, you are free to think."

"Oh!" Nia replied, as if she had stumbled upon an epiphany she had been waiting to set free from her mind. "I guess it makes sense, because I'm always stuck in my room not knowing what to type for my application. It's always a writer's block. But when I ate an apple, I was able to have ideas come into my head even though I was in a *box* or mar-gin—"

"Marginalized."

"Yeah that word! I was marginalized in my room."

"That's true. But remember, this is just my own idea, which doesn't necessarily mean that it's true. What would you do with that idea though?"

"Well, I was thinking about getting outside to finish the rest of my application."

"I'm not mad at that. Remember Nia, you want to always do as much as possible, because if you don't *do*, you'll never know if it's a successful venture. It seems like you're implementing the principles I've instilled in you, and I'm proud of that!"

"Thanks Dad."

"Yup. I'm going to go deeper. Look outside. As I'm driving on these streets, you see all the other people in their own individual cars; they're in their own *boxes* per se."

"Yeah."

"They're all in their own box, marginalized by their own thoughts, but it's conflicting, because they're in a structure where they are protected from the outside world, or outside critiques, since they define their own narrative in their own box."

"Okay?"

"I say this to say that this concept is essentially a commentary on society. Everyone has their own story that's unique to them and as you scan outside, there's a lot surrounding you, but you're protected from it by the marginalization of your own thoughts. It's a matter of whether you're protected or harmed by lack of information and fixation on your own ideals. You be the judge. You define your own world. You define your pace for how you handle your issues."

"I think I kind of get what you mean, but I'll have to try and let that one sink in."

"Yeah, now where you come in is that you have to be in that outside world, consuming other ideas or content for your own creative psyche. That's why I say you're creative. It's like you're a sponge that soaks up information and carries it to greater heights. When you're in a box like a car, your mental frame isn't operating at its highest potential. You've got to know your mind and figure out that relationship you have with it. The mind is a powerful force to be reckoned with. That's just a food for thought."

"My mental frame's potential can be viewed differently in circumstantial situations. I have to establish a relationship with my mind since it's powerful. Interesting."

"Exactly. Now let me tell you one thing about focus Nia. This may sound counterintuitive, but listen! A majority of people will tell you to focus on one thing at a time, because *they* would burn out if they multitasked. Their reality is that by focusing on multiple things at once, failure is imminent *for them* so they attempt to bring you into their reality. Your mindset should be open to receiving failure and embracing it, especially if you want to be equipped to pay off your student loans quickly. Failure should excite you *more* than success because you're one failure away from success. All failure isn't bad, because you can *focus* and *fail*. Listen! Sometimes you want to *focus*, so you can *fail* and learn in order to make adjustments."

They drove the rest of the way in silence. Nia gathered her thoughts. As they arrived at school, she began pondering the accuracy of her father's claims.

"I give up," she muttered to herself. Catching herself quickly as the words left her lips, she reluctantly corrected herself. "It's all mental, Nia. Mental."

She began making her attempt to remove herself from the car. She yearned for the day she would soon drive since she now passed her written exam. Her father stopped her in her tracks.

"Wait Nia! Who are you and who am I?"

"I'm Nia Akintewe, and you're my father who loves me."

"What do you deserve?"

"I deserve all the love in the world."

"What are the three pillars for financial freedom to get rid of your student loan debt or overcome anything you encounter?"

"Believe. Plan. Execute."

"Why should you practice patience?"

"Patience allows me to take risks without repercussions, because it gives me the mindset to focus on the fact I have time."

"And why is gratitude so important?"

"You can't be great without being grateful, it's in the word if you reverse the letters."

Nia pushed her glasses up with her left index and middle fingers as she walked towards the small campus. She stopped by a bench and waited for her class to start, as she noticed various students in her class waiting outside as well. They waited for the current students occupying the classroom to make their exit; such was the cycle of attending college classes.

As she waited, Nia's stomach began to growl. She was more easily agitated these days because she was now always hungry going to class. With that hunger and accompanied sporadic fatigue, her patience was lower than usual. Mindlessly scrolling through applications on her phone, her hands grew sweaty. She lost her grip and it slipped out of her hand, hitting someone nearby. Not making anything of it, she rushed over to grab her phone and apologize.

"Sorry about that!"

The individual that got struck had other plans.

"Why are you so clumsy? Your damn stupid phone hit my new kicks!"

Nia's heart jumped as she looked up to see an angry girl she hadn't seen at school before glaring at her. This girl was fair in complexion enough to get asked questions if she had more than one racial background. Fed up by the fact she was already tired from fasting, Nia had a series of built-up emotions and was ready to retaliate at a moment's notice.

"I said I was sorry! Jeez!"

Nia shook her head as she began walking away. As she made her way to another area to cool down and wait for her class to begin, she felt a sudden push and fell to the ground, collapsing with the ground's surface as her glasses fell off the rim of her nose.

Her heart raced rapidly not because she had been pushed, but for the simple fact her glasses were in danger. She picked them up carefully and noticed it accumulated dust and an insignificant crack on the right lens. Rubbing them with the bottom of her sweater and placing them back on her face, she turned around to view her perpetrator.

It was the light-skinned girl that she mistakenly struck with her phone. Hungry and agitated, Nia used her built up frustration to launch a punch to the tall girl's face, barely connecting with her chin as the girl immediately grew red, retaliating back out of shock and embarrassment.

The girl connected a punch to Nia's chin so potent it tossed her back with momentum, knocking her glasses off her face once more. Nia attempted to scramble for it, but the girl dealt a barrage of mostly missed punches and kicks to her as she now refocused her attention on defending herself. Failing to see accurately, she lodged her own punches and kicks, missing most of them in the process as well. Both attempting to grab one another's hair, they failed to maintain a grip for more than a few seconds. A crowd waiting to enter their class now reevaluated their priorities as they watched in awe.

After a few more strikes from the girl, a bystander appeared out of nowhere, grabbing her. He carried her away from Nia as Nia barely made out the silhouette of the girl striking mid-air while being carried in her attempt to break from the bystander's seemingly binding grip. Nia ceased attempting to defend herself and now scrambled the ground for her glasses. Finding them, she placed them on her face once more and observed the bystander. She quickly realized her savior was the boy in her math class that had drugged her earlier. She now laid eyes on two of her attackers. He carried her perpetrator away whilst the girl still attempted to break free.

"That's why I beat you up! Four eyes! You've got ugly nappy hair! Wipe that dirt off your skin, dirty! You dark skinned lil' bit—!"

The male perpetrator that prevented Nia from being beaten to a pulp covered the girl's mouth, silencing the rest of her obscenities, one attacker silencing another. Nia scanned the surroundings and witnessed many circled around her with flashing phones recording the entire situation. She immediately fled in embarrassment, rushing past people and pushing her way through to call her father to pick her up. School was no longer a priority. College was not necessary.

She called her father promptly and deceived him by stating her stomach was upsetting her; he was quickly on his way. She knew if she informed him what had actually happened he would escalate the situation to levels above a plane's highest altitude. She was drugged in one situation. She felt embarrassed and didn't want to appear weak in front of her father so she protected the information with herself. Besides, she knew if her father knew what that terrorizing character did to her, he was a dead man. She was physically assaulted in a separate situation. She recalled the last time she had been merely verbally assaulted and how it didn't end well for the opposing end, so reporting about being physically assaulted was no better option. She vowed to keep this one to herself as well and recalled how she always carried makeup in her bag. She did this for the purpose of being tossed in any situation where she felt inspired to apply it.

It was her savior today. Nia briskly applied it on her face to conceal the barely noticeable scratches on her face from mostly barely landed punches. She had experienced a series of unfortunate events to the point she was numb to the mental damage sustained from the fight.

"I give up!"

As she arrived in the car, he analyzed her. Nia grew nervous in hope that he wouldn't notice anything different about her. She sat up straight and avoided his eye contact.

"Why are you so tense honey? Relax."

"Oh nothing. Just tired from using the bathroom a lot." She gave off a nervous chuckle. "You know how that goes."

Sustaining slight bruises to her ribs and arms, she was able to conveniently conceal them under her yellow sweater as she endured the Texas heat. As for her face, her father realized she didn't put on makeup often and questioned her.

"Why the makeup?"

Nia grew nervous as she searched for an answer to deflect the question.

"Oh, my stomach was hurting, so I wanted to give myself a reason to feel good about myself by wearing makeup. I'm just practicing self-love." She glanced over at her father briefly. "That's all," she added nervously.

"Oh okay, that makes sense." He directed his attention at her quickly. "You did a great job too sweetie! I used to think you would never wear makeup to be honest."

Despite not feeling mentally distraught from the altercation immediately, her mind still lingered on the fact the girl teased her about her skin being dark. She remembered Kosey's similar judgements and it was like she was reliving those dark days once again.

"But I have a question Dad."

"Shoot."

"If someone thinks they're better than me because they have lighter skin, is that true? And is having natural hair bad?"

Her father grew stern and serious. "What did I tell you about yourself? What do I always tell you about yourself? You are a beautiful, ebony black queen and will be treated as such! You deserve all the love in the world, no matter what shade you are. Don't *ever* think you're less worthy of anything just because your skin is darker than someone else's. Your natural hair is beautiful! I need you to learn to embrace it! You need to dismiss the opinions of people that don't even care about you. Where is all this coming from anyway?"

"Nowhere. Just a quick question I had after thinking about some things."

She flashed back to the fight where the girl chastised her color as if her lighter complexion meant her life was more significant than Nia's. She knew her father preached the importance of not falling victim to the societal group thought surrounding colorism, but it still bothered her sporadically deep down in her faint vulnerability surrounding her skin tone. She thought about giving up once more.

"Well, I hope your stomach starts to feel better. We're going to have to get you in some self-defense classes pretty soon."

Nia's heart raced like a Maserati on its full throttle acceleration.

"W-why do you say that?" She stammered.

He appeared alarmed at her nervousness, but dismissed it. The coast was clear. Her heart found a steady pace.

"I was just thinking about it because everything starts from one's mind. I feel like taking self-defense classes is a great way for you to not only exercise control of your mind, but also be equipped for any creeps when I'm not with you."

Nia's heart picked up once more as she thought about the male in her class that attempted to take advantage of her.

"But I have good news! I'm headed on a speaking gig right now and I have an extra plane ticket if you wanted to come?"

Nia thought about the fact she still had class the next day. Catching herself in her thought, she realized she was thinking in the mindset that she had to return back to where she felt pain. Fed up with everything surrounding school and the idea of college, she figured this was her opportunity to disengage herself away from her problems.

"Yeah! Where is it though?"

"It's in Oregon. It's this place called Klamath Falls. The flight says we are flying to Medford, Oregon."

"Is that near Portland? I've always wanted to go there!"

"No. It's pretty far from Portland actually, but I heard it's on the coast near California."

"Oh! Okay, I guess that's cool too. What about me packing my stuff?"

"Don't worry. I packed you a bag, because I knew you'd want to go."

* * *

As they arrived at the airport, they left their car parked in the lot. They rushed through the TSA process, arriving in line at their gate to check into the plane. Nia was reminded her father was notorious for nearly missing his flights as they conducted themselves with haste. Any trip with him was bound to be a gut-wrenching adventure.

Standing in line, her father played music she couldn't make out as he waited for the line to move an inch. A decrepit, frail pale woman aggressively rushed past him, initiating contact with him despite the fact she possessed adequate space to take an alternative route to pass him. Removing his earphones hastily, Nia directed her gaze his way as she mentally prepared for a scene to commence, but something else occurred.

"Ma'am. You can say excuse me next time. That's all I ask." He made his presence known to her, demanding respect in a respectful manner. She immediately shifted from aggressor to nervous. This was a typical reaction.

Following this situation, they arrived on the plane shortly after. Nia arrived in her seat adjacent to her father, playing the first song her music queue suggested as she revealed her earphones to be unbothered. It was "Blessings" by Lecrae. Aware of the negative stigma surrounding Christian Rap, she wanted to support it and reaffirm her belief, it wasn't subpar music. Not only that, she had a fear of flying on planes, so this was an instinctual, premeditated move as well. She prayed briefly, listened to his music and fell asleep before takeoff.

In the blink of an eye she was awake, experiencing the first bout of turbulence. On top of waking up discombobulated, this wasn't the welcome she wanted to experience, adding to the weighty dilemma. She took out one earphone and glanced over at her father confusedly, assuming they might potentially be in danger. He was calm. This eased her mind. However, he was always calm.

She glanced around and witnessed nearby passengers panicking. Yanking out the remaining earphone that met her ear, her heart began racing as a result of turbulence picking up to astronomical levels. Hearing radio sounds as the pilot was about to make an announcement, she mustered up the little focus she had to pay attention.

"Ladies and gentlemen, I apologize for the lack of communication. Because of the snowstorm going on, I can't see the runway, so I'm going to go ahead and reroute and try and land again. Keep your seat belts buckled. That's all."

Nia was astonished. She traveled from the humid heat in Texas to a violent snowstorm brewing in Oregon. The world never ceased to amaze her. It *was* February. Maybe Texas was the outcast for being humid, while the rest of the world lived in sanity. It was a cold February, but wasn't as cold as the 29th of February.

She glanced over at her father once more and questioned how he remained calm and collected without a regard for their flight conditions. Her newly acquired spiritual mindset convinced her it was due to his strong faith in God; nonetheless she was still shocked.

Nia experienced a mental hiccup. She questioned her faith as she thought her sun could set at a moment's notice, because the plane could potentially crash upon the pilot making any minute error. She began blaming herself for agreeing to attend the trip.

"I give up," she muttered to herself.

Her palms grew sweaty. Her heart traveled like a stampede while she glanced at her composed father once more. She couldn't fathom the fact he was so focused as if the plane wasn't shaking aggressively like a rollercoaster about to detach out of its socket.

"I give up," she muttered to herself once more. "No. It's mental. Don't give up Nia. Keep pushing."

She disregarded her earphones as the turbulence gained more momentum while the pilot attempted to land safely. Glancing out the window, she feasted her eyes on a white, nebulous surface, realizing Texas had skipped the winter that year. The plane continued shaking rapidly as she grew fearful and nauseous.

Nia hadn't vomited since she was a toddler, but the ride felt like the plane was being slapped aggressively by the hand of the bullying wind multiple times. On the third attempt, the pilot made an announcement regarding the runway closure due to inclement weather.

"Because of low fuel, we're going to have to make an emergency stop in Portland. I'm sorry."

The passengers collectively groaned upon the announcement. Another passenger scanned the area, looking around in disgust.

"Y'all should be happy he didn't force a land! That's a life or death thing, you know!"

Nia was torn between happiness and sadness upon realizing the man's point. She didn't know whether to feel happy or sad, because she wanted to go to Portland, but she didn't know if this would be her last flight. She bent her head down and closed her eyes, praying for the best in her attempt to mentally visualize overcoming this debacle.

"I don't know man. I give up."

"Those words you are using," her father began, grabbing her attention. "You gotta be careful with what you say, because the power of the mouth is powerful. You want to prophesy positive things into fruition. You always want to talk about money right? You think saying you give up at paying your debt isn't going to influence your attitude towards your effort?"

"Okay Dad."

"So what's going to happen?"

"We're going to land safely."

"Amen!"

They arrived safely in Portland. It wasn't what she thought it'd be. It looked a lot more boring than she anticipated. As an avid fan of the *Twilight* series, she was aware some of the movie was filmed in Portland. This made her always want to visit, but now she wanted to catch the next flight back to Notsuoh. She was highly disappointed.

The passengers stepped off the plane appearing befuddled and yawning as they made their way to the airport to search for customer service as instructed. Nia's father calmly handled himself as everyone was consumed with negativity, which made Nia question whether or not they flew on the same plane.

"Dad. Were you on the same flight as me, or?"

He calmly glanced at Nia.

"The Lord is my strength! Whatever you ask for in prayer, believe that you have received it, and it will be yours. I asked God for a safe landing and we're here. Simple. How does your name mean purpose, but your prayer lacks one?"

"What do you mean?"

"Why do you pray so much if you don't believe we'll land safely?"

Nia puckered her lips annoyingly realizing her father had made a phenomenal point.

"That's a good question."

They made their way to the front of the line after waiting patiently. They were informed there were no flights back to Medford. Her father looked puzzled.

"And how long will there be no flights? I have a speaking engagement there later today."

"There will be no flights to Medford for the next three days sir."

"Oh. Okay." He grabbed his phone and walked away as he made a phone call to update his client with what had occurred. "Yeah, and they said there won't be any flights for three days, so I'll go ahead and return your deposit to you and I'll figure out a way to get back home." There was a brief pause. "Okay thanks, you too Ron. Bye."

They made their way to nearby seats as their objective now changed. They had to figure how to get back home.

"Dad, how're you so calm and relaxed with all the misfortune that's happening?"

"AQ."

"Huh?"

"We'll discuss it later, let's figure out what to do first."

"Okay? I'm so hungry though." Nia clutched her stomach as it rumbled like a lion's bellowing, the potency of its inflection traveling miles. "But I know that I'm fasting so it's hard and it's only three so I haven't finished for today."

"Go ahead and break it early for today honey. The Lord knows your spirit and mind." Her father chuckled. "He won't be mad at you."

"Okay. Just for today I guess. What time were we supposed to arrive in Medford by the way?"

"A quarter after one." He chuckled once more. "So that tells you the amount of time wasted."

"I knew something was off about this trip. I felt it in my head."

"Yeah, well let's go ahead and get something to eat at this airport before we pass out so we can function and get out of here safely."

Nia closed her eyes performing a quick prayer, and opened her eyes as she nodded her head at her father; they were on their way.

Stopping by the food court, they instantly smelled a distinct aroma that blessed their nostrils. They feasted their eyes on the label: Mo's Seafood and Chowder. They collectively decided to order a burger with accompanying fries. As her father placed their orders, the cashier licked her lips, staring at her father as he glanced up at the menu. She wasn't certain if he noticed, but this woman was undressing him visually.

He ordered a beer as she asked for his identification card and stared at it for a couple seconds.

"Wow!" she exclaimed. "We're basically the same age." She smiled coyly. "You look great for your age!"

"Uh, thank you," he replied, retrieving his card back.

Nia gave the woman a cold stare as they received their food and sat down. Fed up with the idea of someone attempting to flirt with her father, she broke her silence and let out a noticeable groan enough to alert her father.

"Everything alright sweetie?"

"You know that lady was staring at you when you ordered right? She was all licking her lips talking about you look good and blah blah blah!"

"Eh, I think she was just being friendly."

"Dad! She was literally salivating over you."

"Either way, you know I'm not worried about her sweetie. Anyway, you see this situation that happened? *This* is why I'm happy I work for myself as my own boss, because I could have been scrambling telling my boss I have to clock in tomorrow. That idea is dead."

"Yeah."

"I don't have to worry about clocking in and reporting to another grown man to grant me time off, and I create my own schedule." He laughed hysterically. "Heck, I report to myself!"

"Dad, that's why I want to give up and don't know about all this college stuff. I still want to do Computer Science, but I don't know."

"See honey, I went to college though and graduated. It allowed me to have the minimum knowledge base I needed to function as my own boss, so that's where it gets tricky. Sure, there are some that don't need it, but they're outliers. The programming I learned through my Computer Science degree helped me with creating my own website and coding apps I've made profit off of, just to name a few things. Also, don't let me deceive you, there's nothing wrong with having a job, it's just important to own your own business as well as leverage in the case anything negative were to happen with your job."

"Okay, I see Dad. You're right. It's just hard."

"Anything worth having in life is going to be challenging. It's just about how do you *react* to that challenge? That's the key! But you're going to take the day off tomorrow. I thought we would fly back in time peacefully, but because of this situation, I want your mental health to be great so I'm granting you the permission to take the day off. Your mental state of mind is just as important as your physical, if not, more important."

She admired her father's hustle. He did what he wanted and he did it effectively while teaching her principles along the way. Sometimes he was teaching her and she wasn't conscious of the fact she was learning from him. That's how smooth his mentorship was.

He called a hotel nearby and booked it for the night, explaining what had occurred. Successfully accomplishing that, they sat in silence as her father relished in everything that had occurred.

"I'm going to write this situation in my book."

"And I'll be laughing when I read it."

They sat there in silence. Nia suddenly remembered the fact that the Alaska Airlines customer service instructed them to check in with a different Alaska Airlines at the Portland Airport.

"Dad, shouldn't we go see our options with the other Alaska Airlines like they told us to?"

"Oh yeah! You've got a great memory sweetie. Let's go!"

They approached the nearby Alaska Airlines terminal and realized it was empty. They communicated with the agent about their situation and their options moving forward.

"Well, there aren't any other Alaska flights available, but there is a Delta one about to leave at five." The agent glanced over at the clock. "Hmm, it's about 11 minutes to five, but I can call them and let them know you would be coming if that's what you want to do? But you have to act quickly!"

"Yes! We'll take it," they replied simultaneously out of desperation.

The agent called the Delta terminal, notifying the agent about their situation. She printed out a paper and conducted paperwork.

"Okay, you should be good to go."

Nia and her father quickly scrambled to gather their belongings, rushing to the Delta terminal. They sped past people as their hearts were beating aggressively unbeknownst to whether or not they would arrive in time to catch the flight and arrive home sooner.

Huffing and puffing, they arrived at the Delta terminal and noticed no one occupied the desk. Scanning the environment, they glanced out the window and viewed their plane departing, leaving the grasp of their freedom. Unsure of how to proceed, they noticed an agent nearby for a different airline sitting down. He was a Hispanic looking man with innocence emanating from his eyes as he appeared worried upon discovering the disappointment in Nia's eyes.

"I give up," Nia muttered to herself, burying her face in her hands as she smelled grease from the remnants of her French fries.

"Do y'all need any help?"

"Yeah," Nia's father began. "We got moved to this flight," he stated with shortness of breath. "But we see it leaving now so now we aren't sure how to move forward. I see you're wearing a different airline symbol so I'm not sure if you could help us."

"Oh wow! Sorry about that, but yeah I can't help with that unfortunately." He stood up from where he sat and there was barely a noticeable difference. He stood on his tip toes and peered over at the desk where the agent should have occupied. "The Delta agent should be arriving soon and then you can figure out what to do from there."

At a moment's notice, the Delta agent began making his way over to the desk right before they could move another inch. Limping slightly, they were welcomed by an elderly, decrepit pale looking man wearing a confused look on his face. He sported thick bifocals that nearly fell off his face with every limping step he took as he walked with an arched back. He appeared to be having a troubling day, but that didn't stop Nia's father from approaching him and explaining their situation.

"Well you are good for this flight at seven," he began, coughing aggressively in between his words. Nia jumped back attempting to avoid the launched germs spewed. "But you have to go back to the Alaska people since they have the authority for modifications of your ticket. They issued it."

Nia gasped.

"So we have to walk all the way back to the Alaska terminal?"

"Yes ma'am," he replied without looking at her, focusing on his computer screen.

"I give up!"

As they made their way back to Alaska with minimal energy, Nia complained frequently. Her father attempted to dilute the situation.

"You know Nia," he started. "You should think of this situation as a blessing in disguise, because it's an extra reminder that you can be a boss for yourself and determine your own schedule in these kind of situations. It's not bad to work for someone temporarily and absorb the culture and how they conduct themselves as an organization, but I think everyone should own their own business at least. Maximize your earning potential. You can have multiple student loans so why can't you have multiple streams of income and pay it off quicker?" He was breathing aggressively as they walked with a purpose. "The freedom is priceless!"

They quickly retrieved the modification to their tickets from the Alaska agent as they received an apology for the inconvenience. They rushed back to the Delta gate and witnessed the same old man in the distance. Nia stared at him as she attempted to figure out why he looked familiar.

"Oh! He looks like Count Olaf Dad! Doesn't he? You know from a *Series of Unfortunate Events*?" Nia began breathing exaggeratedly. "Kind of like what *we* are going through right now."

Her father laughed hysterically. "Wow! He does look like him. That's funny. I'm surprised I didn't catch that myself. His hairline is all the way back."

"And he has a huge forehead!"

"Classic!"

Nia felt a warm content feeling upon her father validating her, combined with their established rapport. She felt additionally energetic and motivated to continue moving forward in her aspirations. She realized that sometimes she just needed validation from her father in order to keep moving forward.

"You seem happy over there," he began. "I'll give you one nugget really quick. Working relationships are very important to mental preparedness towards taking control of one's mentality, which becomes a byproduct of one's attitude and effectiveness towards paying off any debts they owe. Keep that one."

"Wow! Thanks Dad. Anything else?"

"Don't rush the process, trust the process. Everything we're doing right now is part of the blueprint for that knowledge base. If you're misguided and undecided, knowledge and wisdom can be provided! Believe that wholeheartedly."

They approached the man and he seemed even more bothered than before. It was almost as if he heard their comedic jabs at his hairline. He slowly typed the keys on his keyboard as he processed the printing of their boarding passes. They returned to their departing gate and stood isolated away from the crowd. A man sporting a clean, tailored suit and designer glasses headed in their direction, tossing an exaggerated smile in their direction as they stared at him wondering what he desired.

"Hi! I'm the manager here and I'm aware you were supposed to go to Medford," he began. "We'll get you going in a second here and get your seat taken care of as soon as the other Medford people with an earlier flight get handled. Sounds good?"

He wore a face of deceit behind his attempt at assuring everything would be handled appropriately.

"Sure," Mr. Akintewe replied. Nia understood her father picked up on his unsettling energy by the tone in which he responded.

Nia and her father sat down, waiting for their chance to communicate with an agent and obtain their respective seat numbers. As they sat down for nearly an hour, Nia's father rose up and began performing communicative gestures to himself.

"I know we could get our seats quicker if we go back through TSA. Should I go back to TSA or not? I don't know." He paced back and forth with his hand caressing his chin. "All this stuff is starting to get crazy. Is God playing a joke on me?"

Her father made his way back to the original gate where they witnessed the old man, and Nia followed. She understood her father wanted to discover the man's motive for not assisting them as they were welcomed by the manager wearing his signature face of deceit once more.

"I told Frank over here to go on back to where I originally met you guys and he'll get you handled. Sorry for the delay." He glanced over at Frank typing away slowly. "Frank, why don't you go on ahead and head down over there so you can help these guys out."

"Roger that. I just have one thing to finish and I'll be over."

The manager walked back with Nia and her father. He began sparking meaningless chatter, because he was uncomfortable with the silence Nia and her father were so comfortable with. He was an intruder invading a genuinely silent space.

"You know, this Medford stuff is crazy. There was actually a passenger that was supposed to deliver a eulogy for a funeral out there, but it didn't work because everyone out there was snowed in, and no one can land there. It's so crazy."

"Yup," Nia and her father replied in unison annoyed, illustrated in their avoidance of his eye contact.

Arriving once more at the gate, they took a disappointed rest as they were back to square one. They glanced over as Frank was still typing away. Nia began growing frustrated as she rose up from her seat and scanned her surroundings. She noticed a worker that seemed useful and approached him.

"Excuse me," she began as the man shifted his body facing hers. He was a pale old man with a full head of white hair that looked like he still had a little jump to his step. He appeared less stressed than Frank. "Um, I need my seat printed out."

"Sorry," the man began, with a welcoming voice. "I'm just a lowly flight attendant." He laughed innocently. "I can do nothing for you but pour drinks and give out snacks."

Nia giggled. "Oh I see. Thank you though." She began walking away back to her father. "That work is appreciated though!"

Frank finally made his way over, each step he made a step away from a broken limb. As he arrived, he approached a nearby computer at the pace of a snail and assisted other passengers energetically as he pretended Nia and her father weren't a priority. He continued this method of operation as they rose up and approached his gate. Nia's father chuckled as a result of the matter.

"Are we in the early 1800s? What kind of stuff is this guy doing?"

They glanced over at another gate agent. She was a friendly looking Asian woman and just became free as she finished assisting a customer. She signaled them over and they felt relieved. Nia explained their situation in the form of a tirade as the woman routinely nodded and felt empathetic, stating they would be good without a seat number until the plane boarded. Confused and frustrated, they sat down once more. Nia was beginning to grow impatient beyond measure.

"I...give...up!"

"It's okay sweetie. I get how you feel, but *never* give up. When you quit, *that's* when you've failed."

Basking in his words, Nia sat down in silence for quite some time. Growing impatient once more, she impulsively reacted.

"Dad!"

"I'm right here, no need to yell."

"Sorry. Shouldn't we just take action? Maybe talk to the manager again? This is starting to get old."

"You're right!" He reacted as if she had stated the most brilliant statement he had heard all day.

They rose up equipped with energy to cause mayhem. Her father approached the manager once more as he repeated his same spiel.

"Let me walk you to him. Frank will get you settled over here right now. I apologize for the delay."

"Hopefully," Nia's father replied under his breath in a playful fashion.

The three of them approached Frank; he printed their seating arrangements and handed it to them. It was such an easy process this time that Nia got upset.

"Why was it so difficult to do something so simple?"

"Honey, I ask myself that exact question every single day. *But,* that lets you know some things aren't as hard as they seem when you finally approach it. Take control of your financial situation or anything you approach by attacking it head on and realize it probably isn't as bad as you think it is." He shook his head. "I wish Simba understood that. He would have paid off his debt if he knew it wasn't as scary as it seemed. That's the mind tricking you, and a mindset shift is the medicine for that."

"Yeah Dad," she began in her attempt to avoid appearing overly emotional regarding Simba. "Should we call that hotel you booked and cancel it since we're going to be going home tonight?"

"Wow! You're right! Again!"

Nia's father attempted to call the Portland hotel they had booked for the night to cancel it. Leaving the phone on speaker, Nia heard everything that commenced. The hotel agent declined cancelling their reservation without any additional penalties. Nia's father requested to speak to the manager and the agent placed him on hold briefly.

Time passed gradually as they were on hold for nearly an hour. As the line connected, they were transferred to another phone line and welcomed with a new voice. After explaining their situation and participating in meaningless chatter, they realized they weren't speaking to the manager and it was in fact another employee. They were instructed to be transferred to another line and Nia grew livid.

"Wow, these people are scandalous! That first guy was supposed to transfer us to their manager, but he really had the nerve to trick us with another employee? That's disrespectful! Dad, I don't care anymore. I give up."

"Hey, well on the bright side," Nia's father began. "We are going home." He rose up and went to retrieve an energy drink. It was the first one he had consumed in quite some time and Nia then realized this day had inevitably affected him as well.

As they waited for their flight to take them home once and for all, he took calculated sips from his energy drink.

"Nia, are you familiar with IQ?"

She could smell the fruity smell on his breath.

"Yes Dad, I know what IQ is. Come on. It's that thing that says how smart you are."

"Precisely. Good. What about EQ?"

"I don't know what that is."

"That's fine. Less people know about that one. That's emotional quotient, which is basically your emotional intelligence. It's very important too, but you know what *we* are worried about?" His eyes lit up partly due to the energy boost from the drink and partly due to the excitement he had about the topic of conversation.

"What are we worried about?"

"AQ! This is what I told you about earlier." He noticed a silence about her. "AQ is adversity quotient. Do you know what adversity is?"

"It means any difficulties or hardships you experience."

"Good. Basically like what happened today."

"Okay?"

"My point is," he began with hand demonstrations. "They can have IQ, and they can even have EQ, but we're worried about AQ! Your adversity quotient is very important when it comes to having a growth mindset. It's about answering the question: what difficulties or hardships have you experienced in your life and how did you bounce back from them? It's about, how do you *react* to that failure?"

Nia listened attentively taking mental notes of what her father was spewing energetically.

"You're upset about something that happened to you five years ago and you *still* haven't gotten up? Get up!"

Nia nodded her head to signal she was in accordance with what he was stating.

"With adversity quotient, you can be three things. You can be a quitter, camper or climber. I'm not even going to go in depth about quitters, because that's a waste of my time and energy. Quitters quit." He demonstrated an aggressive illustration as if he threw an object away like a rag doll. "I got them out of the way! That's that."

Nia laughed hysterically. "I don't want to be a quitter if that's how you react to them."

"You don't. Campers are average! You don't want to be a camper, but the sad thing is most people are campers. Campers are envious of climbers and campers are potentially on the verge of being a quitter, or even being a climber. They just fail to execute. They're on the cusp. They fail to realize and have the mentality that having student loans forever isn't a bright idea."

"Wow, that makes sense and that's scary, because a lot of people are campers."

"Exactly! That's why you have to be aware of what you're doing. So you can also be a climber, which is what we are. Climbers climb!" He stretched his arm vertically, pointing his index finger directly upward. "We're trying to get to that mountain! What's your mountain? That's your purpose. That's the mindset to have. Climbers are executors! Climbers don't put themselves in dumb financial situations. They don't go in debt hundreds of thousands of dollars just to get a $30,000 job to show for it. Climbers have role models and mentors that guide them like I'm doing for you so we can prevent that quitter and camper mentality. Climbers constantly have a financial mindset and know their relationship with money. That's the difference in mindset between a climber and the former. Climbers are calculated and have a plan they believe and execute on. Climbers believe, plan and execute!"

"Oh! I'm a climber!"

"Yes you are! You can be a quitter, camper or climber. Remember that!"

They finally arrived on the plane. It began rattling aggressively once more, but they landed safely and arrived home safe and sound. The moment they entered the door, they parted ways to their rooms following such a drastic trip attempt.

Fast asleep, Nia scanned her surroundings and witnessed her failed future-self once more. She smiled as if she was waiting to reconnect with Nia, while Nia emulated her expression.

"Nia," she began. "Like Dad told you, please take those adversity quotient principles seriously! I didn't take it seriously and unconsciously chose to be a quitter, because I dismissed him. I didn't know the importance of mentorship. It's about the importance of knowing someone has been through what you're going through before. I wasn't humble. I was big-headed and thought I knew everything out of immaturity. Someone has paid off their student loans before you. Someone has been a successful Computer Scientist before you. I had so much hatred in my heart for others making a better life for themselves that it got to the point I realized deep down I didn't truly love myself."

"That's scary to hear! Okay. I'll listen to him."

"Please! You must. It's very important that you have the mindset to right my wrongs. All of these problems I suffered from can be attributed to just a simple mindset shift I should have done initially. It's crazy how just the way someone thinks can make or break them. Be a climber, please! You must view difficult differently. View it in the same light that you view what you dislike. If a majority of the world learned to view their student loan debt in that manner, I promise you there would be a significant shift in amount owed."

"Okay wow, I never thought about that, thank you so much! I'll make sure I take that into consideration."

"I mean, you are me. Well, I was you, so I have to look after you for the both of us."

"Anything else?"

"You've completed your first week of fasting. Within the next week or so you'll experience turmoil and may want to give up, but you have to keep persevering and remember that all of this is a mental battle. Your financial obstacles are a mental battle. Don't give up! Do it for Simba! There's a thing called a failure bank. When you give up, you're contributing to your failure bank."

"Noted."

6

EXCUSES

It was now the 14th day of Nia's 21-day fasting journey. She felt amazing knowing her journey was starting to feel like muscle memory. She arrived at the point she felt odd if she didn't eat around the time where she would typically break her fast.

However, despite this breath of fresh air, there was still a luring mental struggle compelling her to invest in the notion of quitting. She was playing mental gymnastics with herself.

Like a thief in the night of her thoughts, she suddenly recalled this novel behavior to likely be attributed to her failed future-self. Nia recalled the warning she received regarding the mental obstacles she would inevitably encounter, and she chose to tighten up for both of them.

"It's the 14th day of this fasting journey," she thought, hoping she reached her failed future-self mentally somewhere in the atmosphere. "I've really been doing this for 14 days straight. I'm really impressed with myself, because usually I would just quit. That's just so easy and this is just so hard. But I have to do it, one way or another."

Despite the conversation she had in her dream with her failed future-self, her mentality towards the idea of fasting was slowly wavering. As spiritually empowered as it made her, she wasn't certain if this unannounced hiccup was a combination of an evil force and self-imposed mental battles, or if it was purely a self-inflicted blow.

"What's the point of fasting if I don't see immediate results anyway? I have to *really* ask myself that question. I haven't really gained anything, I don't think."

She continued playing mental games with herself like two tennis players diligently attempting to beat one another for the prize at the U.S. Open. Uncertain where her mind should be directed, she redirected her mind away from the topic by interacting with her father to obtain his perspective on the matter. She made her way to his room and noticed him listening to an Eric Thomas video. Typical. She recognized it, because she always remembered him watching this specific video: You Owe You. Eric Thomas began his signature inflective speech with passion.

"Well you didn't do what you was supposed to do! So how am I gonna do what I'm supposed to do, for you?"

Glancing at her father nodding and praising ET's words, her eyes meandered near a large box on the ground adjacent to him. The box contained various different colored hoodies. She witnessed her father wearing a pink version. He turned to her and welcomed her with a bright smile full of zeal.

"Good morning sweetie!"

She noticed "190%" and "GoldenOne Dream" in white embroidered letters on the sweaters before answering him. They were delicately folded on top of one another.

"Morning. Why do you have that printed on those sweaters?"

Her father laughed as he retracted exaggeratedly.

"I see someone just woke up and hasn't brushed their teeth yet."

Offended, Nia quickly began to run out of his room to go and brush her teeth, as her father attempted to stop her.

"Wait sweetie! Don't be upset! Everyone gets morning breath, I was just making a little joke!"

She dismissed him as she proceeded to her route. Fuming, she extracted toothpaste on her toothbrush and began brushing aggressively, nearly inflaming her gums in the process. Conducting a thorough brushing, she returned back to her father's room and blew her breath at him.

"How does that smell?"

He laughed once more.

"Minty fresh!"

He redirected his energy towards the television.

"Good. What's that sweater?"

Her father ignored her initially while the video continued playing. He raised the volume and listened to what ET said next.

"Can't nobody stop me but me! You need to get rid of them excuses and you need to stop pointing fingers at people. And you need to start pointing fingers at yourself! What did you not do?"

As the outro music of the video played, he paused the video and gave his undivided attention to Nia.

"So this sweater here is part of my merchandise for my speaking business. When it comes to any business you run, always be of the mindset to try and monetize it through something as simple as merchandise of your movement. Keep the flow of income coming through multiple streams! They give you multiple loans and we take it in a heartbeat." He traced the letters along the pink sweater he was wearing. "190% here on my sweater is basically a mentality I preach about in my speeches. It's a lifestyle for me. As my daughter, it should be a lifestyle for you, the GoldenOne Dream. That's the family business name."

"Wow! Golden...One..Dream. That's interesting. I never even knew that until right now. You're always hiding stuff!"

"Yeah, I usually just keep things to myself, but I'm trying to grow in my mindset. I want to be more intentional about being transparent these days, at least for your sake and your development so you become greater than me and the cycle continues. So the background behind 190%...okay. This is a teaching moment. You ready for what I got for you?"

"Always."

"So you want to have a growth mindset, and with that comes a lot of responsibilities towards achieving this mindset. It's not easy to have. I've said it's easy to say we should have a growth mindset, but executing is the divisive factor. It's not easy to pay off our debts, but executing is the divisive factor. Most of us live in a fixed mindset. 190% is operating at *nearly* twice as good as your best effort."

"Okay?"

"So typically if we give our best effort, we say we gave it 100% right? If we get 100% on a test, we got a perfect score?"

"Yes."

"Well, we're not impressed by 100% anymore. We need to operate on 190% effort and that's the mindset I preach about when I'm traveling around the world speaking to my audience. A lot of kids ask me, 'why not 200%?' And I tell them, when I hear 200% that sounds like two people to me, which is physically impossible for one person, so I went with 190%, because it's what *I* believe in. That's key. It's about what *you* believe in. This is the foundation of living the GoldenOne Dream. You following?"

"Yeah, I think so."

"I think that went over your head. I said I follow 190%, because it's what I personally believe and invest my time in. Remember, you have to believe, plan and execute. My belief is operating on taking control of those spiritual battles I'll encounter along the road towards what I want to accomplish."

"Oh wow! I didn't even notice you said that when you put it like that."

"Yup. So when I'm speaking, I make it a point to distinguish the fact that people that operate at 50% are operating on a fixed mindset, and people that operate on 190% are operating on a growth mindset. This is because the difference between someone that has a growth mindset and someone that has a fixed mindset is that the fixed mindset person does not know their self, while the growth mindset person knows their self. 190% means that they're operating on their full potential, because they know their worth. 50% is half of what is deemed our best effort, so those people are operating on a fixed mindset, because they aren't giving their full potential."

"I'm following you Dad."

"Good! One trick I use to make sure I'm operating in a growth mindset is meditation. Do you meditate sweetie?"

"No."

"I know, I just wanted to ask." He laughed. "Well, meditation is powerful, because it's a means of taking control of not only your mental battles, but your spiritual ones as well. You can look at it as a two birds-one stone situation. You can even argue it takes control of the physical battles we encounter in life."

"That's amazing!"

"Indeed. I encourage you to place an emphasis on high value of return activities versus those that have a low value of return in order to be maximally productive."

"What does that mean?"

"Perform passionate activities that give you a high return of value to your life. This is why I meditate, because it has a high value of return in boosting one's creativity and focus as opposed to a low return of value activity like using all your time to watch television, which can infiltrate your mind for an imminent failure. That's why I read so much, because it's a high return on your investment. Use your time wisely is what I'm saying.

"But with meditation, we have to compare it to medication for emphasis of its power. When I say medication, I'm talking about self-medication like drugs you shouldn't be doing." He oscillated his hands, placing one hand noticeably elevated above the other. "Medication, medicate. It's this one down here. Meditation, meditate. That's this one up here."

"Okay, what does that mean though?"

"This should look familiar about what I talked about earlier. Look at this lower hand I have right here. This is a fixed mindset, 50% effort and medication. Look at this higher hand I have here. This is a growth mindset, 190% effort and meditation. It's really a simple concept when you break it down like this."

"Wow! I agree. That's a great way to look at it!"

"This right here is a gem Nia. I would listen and write this down if I were you! Listen!"

"I'm listening."

"Medication is a temporary feeling," he began, pausing dramatically. "And meditation is permanent healing!"

"Now that's a message!"

"It couldn't be anything else, sweetie. So that's just a little breakdown of what I talk about and my purpose of the 190% merchandise. I fully believe in it in my spirit and I use daily meditations and reading consistently to leverage my mental prowess and keep my mental struggles in check."

"Interesting. I wanted to ask. What about the GoldenOne Dream? What's that?"

"I could start talking about that now and we wouldn't finish for another year, but I'll do my best to keep it simple."

"That's preferred," she replied chuckling.

"Okay. GoldenOne Dream is a revolutionary lifestyle I've founded. It's my movement and I believe in it wholeheartedly. It's where I get the three-step process of believing, planning and executing from. GoldenOne Dream's acronym is GOD, because God is prioritized first; that's the belief aspect and spiritual control. It's also about taking control of mental struggles one encounters through things like meditation and reading like I just told you. That's why I've been intentional on you about reading. And then arguably the most important part is taking control of physical struggles through execution. It took me a while to realize this, but these three foundational steps of GoldenOne Dream are the three steps I took to take control of my student loan debt at a rate faster than my peers. I unintentionally performed these three steps and saw results, so if I can make you aware of them consciously and be intentional with it, the world better be prepared for Nia!"

"Thanks Dad! That's pretty cool that's the acronym for it too!"

"Yup. My mindset when I founded it was responding to the concept of the American Dream. It's my twist on it. I feel like lately there's been a confusion about what it means to be an American since a lot of crazy divisive stuff has been going on throughout the nation. As a response to that, I founded GoldenOne Dream as a space for minorities alike, and even members of the dominant society that aren't poisoned by prejudice in their ways, to thrive. I feel like anyone can be a golden one without a luring question. That's my play on those words, and a lifestyle I fully embrace. I know it'll reach and resonate with millions of people long past our lives."

"That's so amazing and inspiring Dad!" Her father observed the burning passion to succeed in her eyes. "How do I start my own business?"

"Well first, if you already have your business idea down, I would recommend you get an LLC."

"LLC? What's that?"

"It's called Limited Liability Company and basically establishes your business as an official company while protecting your personal assets. It's a necessity to any business. If you don't have an LLC, you don't exist. My company is GoldenOne Dream LLC. I'm protected and relevant."

"Can you elaborate?"

"Okay. I'll be getting revenue from selling my merchandise and I'm making money from that and everything else I do related to my business. Let's say someone doesn't like what I'm doing and decides to sue me. The purpose of the LLC is to protect my personal assets or what I own and the business is responsible for the damages, so it's essentially like insurance."

"Oh wow okay, that's cool."

"They didn't teach me that in school! I'll keep that in mind. I don't have a business idea yet though. I just got excited."

"That's fine," he replied, giggling at her remark. "There's a lot of stuff they don't teach you in school sweetie, but you have to ensure you invest in yourself and learn on your own. Education is key, no matter how you acquire it. You have to continue to realize, these schools are businesses as well and if they can capitalize off millions of students being ignorant about debt, they will, and they'll continue to do so year after year and semester after semester. Lucky for you, you have an advantage with me mentoring you throughout the process.

"Mentorship is very important, because there's always someone that's already experienced what you're currently experiencing, and they can guide you further along than you would go on your own. That's partly why they say ego is the enemy, because those that allow their ego to infiltrate their mind won't step down and allow another more experienced person to come in and take control of the situation for the greater good. Ego is in cahoots with boredom. Remember these are all illnesses contributing to the ploy of their father, failure."

"That's like the Mastermind Napoleon Hill talked about because we're all trying to accomplish the same goal!"

"Yeah, similar concept. But one thing to remember while we're on the topic of business is to remember the relationship between engagement rate and followers."

"What's the relationship?"

"I know you're a social media fiend. When doing business with others, remember there's a difference between followers one has versus how many people are engaging with their content. A lot of people satisfy their fragile ego by buying followers and having millions of followers, but they only have 100 people engaging with their content. You want to focus more on engagement rate than the number of followers you have.

"Communicate with and engage with those that are your core followers, or teammates like I say, as opposed to worrying about the number of followers. Those will come when you engage with the former first. All of this stuff is a mindset shift. Your mind has to be *wired differently* in order to be successful. Your mind has to be *wired differently* in order to pay off your student loans unbelievably quickly. I'm not telling you to pay it off quickly like me, but be of the mindset that having student loans for a long time isn't your reality. You define your story. Our society tends to romanticize having student loans for decades as a reality for some strange reason." He placed his finger on his temple aggressively. "The mind is the beginning point and catalyst for irrefutable change. Remember that."

"Okay Dad, but now that you say that, that reminds me of something. One thing I heard about is paying influencers a little bit of money to sponsor a product I have to reach more people and reach more sales. Is that a good idea?"

"Exactly! It sure is a great idea, for now. The thing is, most people don't recognize the fact that influencer marketing and having ads on social media is extremely cheap right now. We're in 2025. It's going to be extremely expensive down the line so take advantage of it right now!"

"Okay Daddy. But I came here to ask you something else. How come other people that don't do a 21-day fast get things easily and I'm doing it and still struggling in life? What's the point?"

"Nia," her father began as she knew he was serious from calling her name.

"You have to have the mentality to worry about yourself and yourself only. That's the way your brain has to operate to not get consumed by the outside noise. This disciplined effort is important when you're learning to take control of your mental battles. This is why I meditate."

"But even when I try and focus on myself, I think about what other people are doing. If it isn't that, I'm thinking about myself and creating excuses for myself to quit. I'm not sure how to get out of that spell. Maybe meditating will help me."

"Believe, plan and execute. This is where plan comes into play. Stretch your mind by creating a plan. Create a plan for how you want to do everything you want to do. Creating a written plan is effective, because once it's written, you just have to follow it. People forget things, but words on a paper don't forget anything. You've already mastered the first pillar of GoldenOne Dream in my opinion, the belief pillar. After that, there's the plan phase, which is what you are on right now as far as I'm concerned. Create a written plan and value your time. People that have less time on their hands are more productive, because time is valued as a finite resource. This is where the business intelligence comes in. This philosophy can make or break a business. That's something to think about."

"I can't do it."

"You sound 50 feet!"

"What?"

"I knew that would grab your attention! That's just an inside joke my colleagues and I used to use in school. If you put 50 right next to the abbreviated version of feet like they're all one word, it looks like the word, soft. So I said you sound 50 feet, which means you sound soft. We were coding an assignment one time and outputted a code for that and made it an inside joke."

"Dad, you're a nerd and 50 feet but I still can't do it." Nia sighed heavily. "I fear failure and success because...I give up!"

"Excuses! Excuses! Didn't you just say you were making excuses for yourself to quit? That sounds like more excuses to me!"

"But I can't do—"

"That's disrespectful to the opportunity you've been blessed with!" He yelled aggressively grabbing her, as beads of sweat trickled down his face, saliva projecting from his mouth. "What did I tell you about saying you can't do something? Never say you can't do something! *This* is why we do our affirmation routine! You're messing up the brand when I'm going around the world inspiring people. How does it look if I can't even maintain that inspiration within my own household?"

"I know you said not to say that! I'm not dumb! It's just the way I am!"

"Well then you need to *fix* the way you are!"

"Why would I *fix* the way I am if you're always talking about this stupid fixed mindset stuff being so bad?"

Her father took a deep breath and calmed down.

"I'm sorry sweetheart. I just wish the best for you."

Nia emulated his demeanor.

"It's okay, Dad. I know."

They cooled down for a couple minutes, awkwardly not knowing how to continue their conversation. Nia's father broke the utter silence.

"Like I was saying, you want to create a plan for any and everything, whether it be to pay off debt or get from point A to point B. It can serve as a means of reframing your mindset and giving you that necessary *control* over the mental battles you struggle with. Okay, let me break it down in terms of the mindset and plan I used for paying off my student loan debt since I know that's what you're interested in. You'll need this knowledge since you'll have student loans."

"Okay great! You know I've been waiting for this financial stuff! Any tips on paying it off quickly would be amazing."

"I know, and I think we're at that point for you to understand. You understand the prerequisite information I mentioned a while back.

"Anyway, I have a theory. Being descendants of a hunter-gatherer society, as humans we aren't wired to save. The concept of saving or saving money requires an override of our natural conditioning as humans. We've got to accept the 'tragedy' per se, of being human and know that we have the power to reframe our mind. Remember that. You have the power to reframe your mindset. So in simpler terms, paying off your student loan debt quickly is a mindset shift that you have to initiate for yourself. You can say you'll do it and know that it's a mindset shift, but you have to *apply* what you're preaching. Application is execution! So many people read without applying what they're reading. That's why execution is the most important piece of the GoldenOne Dream triangle."

"Okay, that's interesting. Continue!"

"Yeah. So one thing that helped me pay off my debt I had quickly is just accepting the fact that we are lazy as a society. That's a reality check. Some of us allow food to determine our financial situation. That needs to be fixed for the purpose of growth. Some of us allow our insecurities to determine our financial situation, because we buy things to impress people that don't care about us. All that needs to stop! It's like, you're not worried about how *you* view yourself?"

"I agree Dad," Nia stated, looking down as she took notes in her phone.

"Just a side note, your most important wealth building tool is your income, so when you don't owe anyone any money, you can begin building wealth and focusing on generational wealth. A lot of people think that nothing is wrong with paying off student loans forever, but that's just a crazy way of thinking! That's why I talk and yell about these growth mindset topics, because having a growth mindset is that mindset shift you need to pay off your debt quickly! You might hear me and think I'm just yelling about this growth mindset stuff to just tell kids to do better in their classes, or help you muster up the confidence to become a Computer Scientist. No! It's deeper than that!"

"That's very true. I guess I thought about it on a surface level. But also, I think it's just cool to have financial freedom. I didn't want to carry around my student loan debt initially, but I didn't really consider the unconscious effect of taking years to pay it off so I'm glad you're giving me the resources as a financial consultant."

"I like that you say that sweetie, but I don't think consultant is the right word. I would call myself a financial coach, if anything, because a coach helps you recognize your genius and unlock what you already know; I'm helping you tap into your untapped potential by laying out an effective blueprint that I used to pay off my own debt very quickly. You already know this stuff from within Nia, I'm just helping you extract it out of your mind. Everything starts from the mind so that's my focal point for your development; remember that."

"Okay. Financial coach? That makes sense though."

"Yup. Anyway, another thing that's important about paying off your debt quickly is recognizing your own specific 'why' and operating on it. It's the same thing as being a climber and going up the mountain. Why do you want to pay off your student loan debt? That's a question you should ask yourself. What's your why?"

Nia paused, wondering if this was a trick question.

"Well, I want to be debt free and have financial freedom."

"Okay, that's great Nia, but that's a generic answer that everyone tends to state. There's nothing wrong with that, but I ask that question because a lot of people are surface level like that and can't even answer that simple question. That's the first place to start instead of making blanket statements about wanting to pay off your loans because it sounds cool.

"This process really travels deeper than just alleviating the burden of these loans for good. If you can't answer that question deeper than what you just said, you need to do an evaluation of how serious you are about paying off your debt. My 'why' is because I didn't want a negative net worth and wanted to own my dollars to start the wealth building process. Also, I wanted to impact my community by helping others do the same through helping them recognize their potential as a financial coach."

"That's a deep answer Dad!"

"Yeah, and you may not know it, but I coach clients from time to time and help them get rid of their debt. It's so amazing when my strategies click with people and they recognize on paper that they can do it. Remember what I said about writing things down? It's amazing showing them their true potential that's untapped. That coaching session with me is powerful because it's not only about realizing their potential, but it's also about accountability.

"I will harass my clients into success by constantly making sure they're doing what they promised they would do. It's tough love, but they'll be giggling when they build wealth! It's my goal to make each and every one of my clients, no matter what race, religion or creed, live the GoldenOne Dream!"

"That's so amazing Dad! I didn't know you had some cool things like this going on with you! Now I see what you're up to when I'm at school. You seem to just move in silence."

"Yeah." Her father laughed. "Well, continuing on, it's about a lifestyle change. Getting rid of debt is a lifestyle versus a diet. So when I tell you this lifestyle, you'll want to make sure that you keep repeating it even after you become debt free. By the time I'm done helping you, you're going to live a permanent lifestyle of someone that is mentally framed to be wealthy, the GoldenOne Dream lifestyle."

"Okay Dad, I'm all ears. I'm excited!"

"So this lifestyle includes what you kind of have already been doing anyway, but I'm just here to help you tap into it and actualize it. It starts with taking control of these spiritual, mental and physical battles you encounter. Remember to believe, create your plan, and execute it. For me personally in getting rid of my own debt, to take control of the spiritual battles, I followed God to maximize my spiritual strength. Fasting like you are doing currently is an excellent way to take control of that! Evil forces don't like great things so you have to continue to implement prayer as a weapon and take control of the spiritual phase!"

"Okay, thanks!"

"Anytime sweetie. Take control of the mental hiccups you encounter. I read daily and meditate to maintain my mental acumen. So many people physically workout, but you need to mentally workout too and that's where meditation comes in. I think meditation will help you with the excuses that are constantly infiltrating your mind. Taking control of the physical battles encountered just comes down to execution. I exercised consistently to maintain an optimal frame and operate on an effective mental state to make sound decisions based on my spirit. Do you see how the phases coexist and mingle with one another? Take control of those three battles and you are not only equipped with the tools necessary to take on any debt you accrue, but a byproduct is adopting a growth mindset. That's the GoldenOne Dream!"

"That makes sense," Nia began, typing away aggressively in her phone. "It seems like everything is starting to align and come together."

"Giving!"

"Giving what?"

"You've got to be a go-giver before a go-getter. Give before you get. I'm not talking about giving more money to churches, but I encourage you to give to those in need, whether it be financially or something else. This is important to the lifestyle, because the law of attraction is alive and well. I think so. The more you give out into the world, the more you'll receive in return. Don't give to get though. Give with effort and discipline! When you give, you'll succeed! There's power in being genuinely selfless."

"Okay, that makes sense."

"Affirmations. I believe in daily affirmations, because it's the power of speaking things into existence. The power of the mouth is powerful, so you want to prophesy your dreams into fruition! This is why I constantly talk with you and affirm you whenever I can, because you need to realize your worth and recognize that you are a beautiful, young black queen."

"Oh wow, thank you Dad! That makes sense now why we do that. I didn't even think about it, but even though some days I don't like doing it, it's definitely helped my confidence over the years, and I notice it more now as I'm on this fasting journey and trying to take control of my mental obstacles. I've even embraced my natural hair now too!"

"Yup, that's right and I'm glad you're seeing the effect. Also, consider executing 30 day challenges, because that's powerful as well. Something like omitting fast food for the month sporadically can perform wonders on your student loan debt. I'll help you out with that as you get more debt, but this is preliminary information I should have laid out for you when you were in high school, but better late than never. You're still early anyway, because I didn't learn this until I was about to graduate. Besides, I lay out this information for adults older than me, because taking control is a skill that doesn't discriminate by age, so everyone can learn something from what I'm spewing.

"Also, tell your money what to do! I know you can't relate yet, but control it like it's your child! That's a mindset shift I had to make early on to alleviate myself of my debt. This is why I always talk to you about identifying your relationship with money. You want to ask yourself: what's my relationship with money?"

"Noted."

"It's very important to define your relationship with money, because you have to remember that money is an abundant resource. You should never allow money to take control of your life when there is so much of it out there. That's my relationship with money. It is abundant and I don't dwell on losing it. I would lose it all without losing sleep. I had to realize this when I paid off my debt quickly. Most people have an unhealthy relationship with money, because they clutch it like it's their last. It may be their last, and that's only because they're enslaved mentally. There's always more money out there to be acquired."

"I wish we could have told Simba that," Nia replied staring at the ground. She picked her head up quickly realizing she had grown acclimated to his death.

"Keep your head up sweetie! Yeah, I know. No one knew he was going through, but it would have helped him if he established a healthy relationship with money. Money is an infinite resource! Most people believe it's a finite resource, but when you know in your mind, body and soul you can always get more, you'll be more willing to invest in yourself and succeed. It takes spending money to make more money. You don't become rich by saving money. Wealth is a money generation game, and spending is an instrument for accomplishing that."

"That's interesting. I did promise myself I wouldn't allow money to do that to me after what happened to Simba, but it's interesting realizing why most people don't invest."

"Average people don't invest in themselves, because they clutch their dollar like it's their last, which is sad but true. Oh!" Her father grew excited. "I almost forgot another thing for my lifestyle change I had to grasp. This is a tough pill to swallow for a lot of people, but listen to me.

"It's important to have fun and treat yourself, but the issue is that most people have *too* much fun! Don't get me wrong. Play and fun is important for brain development, because it helps with brain plasticity, planning and prioritizing so we have to have fun, but don't be excessive. I happen to be an outlier predicated off of the fact I'm simple and don't require spending money to have a lot of fun. That has to be taken into consideration about my advantage at paying off my loans quickly too. You're my daughter, so I wouldn't be surprised if you have that financial advantage as well."

"Okay thank you so much Dad! Hopefully I do! Wow, this is a lot of great information and a lot to take in at once!"

"It is, but don't worry, I'll always be by your side, so if you need me to repeat things years from now I will. You have to always remember you have an advantageous assistance with me guiding you, because accountability is huge." He winked at Nia. "So don't disappoint kiddo."

She hugged him and grew emotional. "Wow, I'm so lucky." Tears began falling fluidly, streaming down her face. "I love you Daddy."

He placed a kiss on her forehead. "I love you too sweetheart."

He separated from her and wore a confused look as if he was pondering something to tell her next.

"Why that face Dad?"

"I was just thinking," he began. "Okay, I think that was basically the lifestyle change I made. Those were the things I had to be aware of mentally to get to the next level, but I have a question now for you."

"Shoot," Nia replied laughing, imitating her father's signature response when she had a question for him.

"We've got a comedian over here I see. But, would you rather make $50,000 and everyone around you makes $25,000? Or would you rather make $100,000 and everyone around you makes $200,000?"

"Hmm," Nia began, her finger placed on her chin in deep thought. "I'll take the $50,000."

"Wrong!" he stated with incredible inflection ringing through her ears.

"Whoa," she replied jumping back startled. "Why is that wrong?"

"You need a reality check sweetie. You need to worry about yourself, and that's the reason why I asked that question."

"What do you mean? I don't want the people around me to make more than me?"

"See? That's insecurity! A lot of us are surrounded by an egotistical mindset and we want to make it seem like we're better off than everyone around us, even if it means going to the extent of compromising our own success. Worry about yourself! You'll be driving very soon, and this is why they tell you not to rubberneck. You know from your test that means looking over at someone else driving when you should worry about yourself and your road."

"Wow, great analogy. I guess that's true."

"Think about it. I gave you two options. You would choose to receive half your earning potential just because making more money than those around you would stroke your ego? I said ego is the enemy earlier! You can't accept others around you doing slightly better if it means you'll be successful in your own right? That's insecure! Ask yourself that question."

"Wow! You're right Dad. I didn't even think about it like that. I understand now though."

"Yup. Just a little quick hack. I recommend you pay off your debt biweekly, because when you do that versus monthly payments, you're making an extra payment that sneaks in after a year. You're paying the same amount of money regardless, so you might as well take advantage of that. Your payments are accounting for 13 months versus 12 months if you do monthly. Write it down on paper if you don't believe me."

"Wow! I believe you. That's another great nugget. Thanks Dad!"

He placed his index finger on his temple. "The power of thinking." He grew slightly emotional. "Your mother taught me that one."

Nia mirrored his sadness and took a deep breath to catch herself in her pursuit to stay composed. Her father sniffed and was back to normal. She mirrored him once more.

"Okay, let's discuss budgeting. A lot of people hate that word, but more than likely, you're going to have to budget in some capacity. Keep that in mind and embrace it."

"I have to view difficult differently."

"Exactly! So a budget isn't necessary because you can simply spend less than you make if you're wired that way. Most people aren't wired that way, so a budget is one convenient means to keep order. A budget is only one means, because it can be done multiple ways, but remember it's just convenient. This goes back to the power of writing things down into existence. Got it?"

"Yes sir!"

"Good! I love that energy. The main principle about a budget you need to know is: know what your money is doing and take control of it. Like I said, control it like it's your child. Everything I'm telling you is about the relationship between control and mindset."

"I understand. I have to take control of my mindset. Got it!"

"You're getting it! One more thing about budgeting before I forget. Budgeting to most people is like dieting, because you can do it until you're debt free and then quit. The solution is permanently living the lifestyle I've told you about."

"Okay, I got that down. Is that it?"

"Nope! If you can't tell me by the dollar and cents what you spent on groceries or fast food three months ago on a specific date, then we have an issue. Budgeting is about the pain of discipline versus the pain of regret!"

Nia glanced at her father whilst taking notes, noticing he dramatically paused.

"Okay."

"I'm going to repeat myself since that didn't impress you. Budgeting is about the pain of discipline versus the pain of regret, so do what you gotta do!"

"Oh my gosh Dad, you're so extra!"

"Extra-ordinary. Extraordinary! You want to think about your budget as your business. You are the CFO—"

"What's the CFO?"

"Chief Financial Officer. Based on your money management, would you fire yourself today or keep yourself employed? *That's* the mentality you need to have when it comes to getting rid of your debt. Write that down."

"Noted."

"Also, patience is key! You have to be patient! I'm repeating myself again. You *have* to be patient if you want to be successful with paying off your loans or attacking any issue you come across. This is why I make it a point to remind you with our affirmation routine. It took you 17 years to be 17. Don't rush the process, trust the process!"

"You're *so* right! It's hard for me to be patient because I want things right away, but I'll do my best."

"Patience is important because it allows you to be a risk taker without taking on any repercussions, because you're granting yourself the mindset shift to understand that you've got time. That's why I ask you that in our routine. Everything starts from the mind sweetie! If you don't remember anything that I tell you, please remember that.

"Alright, I don't want to talk your ear off, but I'll just give you one more nugget. With creating your budget, you want to do a screening process where you identify your needs and wants and categorize them. Some of these needs can be bills or rent."

"What about junk food?"

"Not so fast. That's a 'want' item ma'am!"

"Oh dang."

"Yeah, so when you do that you can create your budget in an excel sheet, write it down physically or use one of those technological interfaces y'all kids use these days. Any of them are powerful, because they're all written or documented. Maktub. You decide your fate."

"Okay, what does that word mean though?"

"Maktub. It's Arabic for, 'it is written' and on that note, I have a book to recommend you. You don't have to get it right now from my library, but I want you to read Paulo Coehlo's *The Alchemist* so you can be familiar with the fact that there's power in passion, but there's even greater power in purpose! Reading this book was a prerequisite of building my character to alleviate my debt. It's a very important read that facilitated my pursuit towards a growth mindset and I feel honored to be able to share it with you. Understanding the relationship among power, passion and purpose will grant you an additional avenue for fostering a growth mindset. You were named Nia for a reason, so start acting like it!"

Nia rolled her eyes.

"Here we go again."

"Ain't no 'here we go again' in here. I don't want to hear any more excuses from you okay? You have the gift and knowledge base to do it, you just need to do it. You simply needed the coaching to help you realize and tap that untapped potential. You understand me?"

She bowed her head down, avoiding his gaze while sighing.

"Yes Dad. I'm excited to read *The Alchemist* though!"

"Good. Now give me a high five!"

They joined hands emitting a powerful noise of financial freedom.

"How's the fasting going?"

"It's going great and I'm not complaining or using any excuses anymore. Right Dad?"

"Right! But I can't emphasize enough how powerful *Think and Grow Rich* is. Did we ever get to talk about it? I don't think I told you about my favorite part."

"No we didn't but I agree!"

"Okay perfect! There was a part where he said something like, 'I realize that thoughts become reality and I'll spend 30 minutes each day focusing on creating a clear mental picture of the type of person I must become in order to achieve my goals.' That was fire!"

"It was! There were so many things in there I wanted to highlight, I almost had to highlight the entire book!"

"Exactly! I say that to say that Napoleon Hill was talking to you when he wrote that! Eradicate all excuses! Meditate daily and view yourself having that growth mindset! The mind is powerful and can achieve unbelievable things! Meditate daily and view yourself getting over your fear of public speaking and *becoming* a public speaker and motivating others!"

"I don't know about that one," Nia replied unenthusiastically disgusted at the thought of being a public speaker.

"Nia, you should know as much as I do since you read that book. The mind is very powerful and has no limitations. The mind is responsible for the conquering of these spiritual, mental and physical battles. The mind leads to having an optimal mind frame to pay off any debt and maintaining a growth mindset as a byproduct of being wired in that way. And *my mind* tells me that your main struggle right now is dealing with controlling the thoughts in *your mind* and overcoming those tough mental battles. The mind is scary."

"Wow Dad! It's like you're in my head or something. How do you know?"

"I do this mindfulness stuff sweetheart." He smirked arrogantly. "I've been doing it for a while. When you're consistent at something, I would hope that you would get better over time."

"I'm trying to get like you Dad."

"Aw, I'm so flattered." He embraced her with a hug. "One more thing now. I need you to do me a favor and repeat after me, okay?"

"Got it."

Before her father could utter another word, they heard a voice from the television as a beat entered the room. It was "Mind Playing Tricks on Me" by Geto Boys and Nia's father nodded his head to the beat elated. Nia was confused.

"Who is this?"

"This is Geto Boys, with Scarface! This is a really good song. You should listen to the lyrics since you're going through a lot of mental struggles right now. They're talking about paranoia and anxiety within the mind. I can't tell you enough how powerful the mind is Nia. You may not have consciously realized, but it can play tricks on you. Simba's mind was playing tricks on him unfortunately. Take control of your mindset."

"Who's Scarface?"

"Just repeat after me and listen to the song after," he replied shaking his head.

"Okay Dad," she replied chuckling.

"I, insert your name, vow to not have excuses anymore and I rebuke them!"

"I, Nia Akintewe, vow to not have excuses anymore and I rebuke them!"

"Good! Good!"

With that being said, Nia felt content with finishing up the last seven days of her fasting journey. She listened to the lyrics of the song, attempting to take control of her mind and escape the tricks she had failed to realize had transpired when she lost her focus. The finish line was fast approaching and she could see it clearly now, mentally.

7

WITH EFFORT AND DISCIPLINE!

It was day 21. The final day of the journey Nia had worked so diligently to complete. There was no turning back now. Undergoing an entire week of intentionally omitting excuses from her language and digesting the contents of *The Alchemist* and its worship of pursuing one's personal legend, she felt spiritually strong, but mentally stronger. She was now in her element more than ever. As someone that often would start something and quit shortly after, she was surprised with the progress she made for herself.

Feeling lovely, she gracefully made her way to the living room where her father resided. She aimed to make her presence known and participate in any type of conversation, because she was on an emotional high, being it was the last day of her lengthy journey. As she maneuvered towards the living room, she heard an aggressive, consistent tapping sound as her father was typing rapidly; each finger stroke on the keyboard nearly sent the keys flying out of their sockets. She stood in place noticing he was extremely focused, but decided to interrupt him briefly, maneuvering her way in his field of vision.

"Hey Dad!"

"What's up sweetheart," he glanced up, acknowledging her briefly but returning his vision back to his laptop screen. "I'm working on this book right now, *The Power of Yet*. I think it's going to be a game changer. I knew that had to be the title when you mentioned it that day at the dinner table."

"Hey! You're plagiarizing my ideas!"

He smirked without moving an inch. "Maybe I'll dedicate it to you. But the book is basically following my most popular speaking topic, growth mindset. It's about going from a fixed mindset to a growth mindset. That principle is the overall theme, but it's deep, because the principles I lay out in the book are pretty much a blueprint for why I was able to alleviate any debt I accrued so quickly, so I'm excited to share this timeless piece with the world."

"Are you sure it's *not* going to be like the other one that never came out?"

"Yes I'm sure!" He balled his hand into a fist and shook it at her laughing. "You think you're so funny don't you? But I'm definitely more passionate about this one and wholeheartedly believe in the principles I've illustrated. I just wrote the last one to try and assimilate with what was popular. The writing process was easier this time around, because I actually believed in what I was typing."

Nia chuckled. She glanced over his shoulder as she witnessed he had over 100 pages typed. Shocked, she wondered how he was able to accomplish such a feat in a small period of time.

"How did you even write a book?"

"I just typed it?"

"I mean...how were you able to do it, because I feel like writing a book is so hard."

"With effort and discipline!"

"That's it?"

"That's it! Well, with a little bit of consistency. But effort and discipline is the main formula I used with this one. I did that with the last one, but I didn't care about the last one, so that was the missing formula. You have to care about any service you're providing to the world if you want them to care about what you're putting out."

"That's incredible. That seems so simple."

"Well, when you think about the question you asked me, that's simple as well isn't it? Writing a book seems like putting words on paper, but there's a certain savvy art to it. There's also a certain savvy art to effort, discipline, and genuinely caring."

"Can you elaborate on that? I feel like this is a teachable moment again. Am

I right?"

"Right for once," he answered, fixing his gaze on her while he revealed his index finger in a vertical stance.

"Hey! I'm always right Dad. I don't know what you're even talking about!"

"Whatever helps you sleep at night sweetie. I don't want you up not getting full rest, so I'll agree to disagree. Speaking of sleep, just a side note, I always ask you the number of hours you slept, because you can't be great if you don't sleep!"

"Oh wow! Okay. Sometimes I get annoyed when you ask like you're trying to spy on my sleep."

"No. I'm just genuinely concerned about your health, because I've witnessed so many successful people spew out this notion that you have to be up 24/7 grinding as if they don't hire people to do work for them and get their own fair share of sleep. You can't do everything."

"I'm listening."

"You have to sleep! Sleep is part of the grind! I'm going to repeat myself. *Sleep* is part of the grind! All that advertising of grinding being aligned with lack of sleep isn't a good thing and the rich say it to stay ahead of the rest of the world. Our society romanticizes the idea of avoiding adequate sleep and I'm tired of it. Nia, you *must* sleep and get enough of it!

"Lack of sleep can literally kill you. I've seen it happen to my peers. You wouldn't think so, but it's true. In our community, there are a lot of people subject to hypertension and that's because they focus excessively on the 'grind' and forget sleep is literally grinding as well. When you get enough sleep, you're grinding correctly. That's a part of the GoldenOne Dream lifestyle that helped me pay off my loans quickly. I slept and had a sound mind to make logical decisions."

"Oh wow Dad. I thought you were someone that didn't sleep much, because I always see you up early, but that's crazy how we're fed that idea in society."

"I wake up early, because I sleep early. That's the consistent discipline. Keep the same energy on both fronts. Also, when you don't sleep you potentially can kill yourself by 40 years old, and when it's all said and done, the average person that got enough sleep that lives twice that age potentially made more money and had more time to grind than the person that focused on 'grinding' too much without sleep. Remember that."

"I understand."

"Anyway, like I was saying earlier, there's an art to applying effort and discipline with your aspirations, because it's only optimally effective when you've set forth your plan. Remember that plan stuff I was telling you about last week? It's about mental control."

"Okay, I believe I'm following."

"I set forth a plan and gave myself a deadline and laid out the timeline for how I wanted everything to progress throughout the journey. Being in book mode is obviously not an easy task, especially when I have a lot of other things going on, but I made it an actionable step in my plan to eradicate all excuses. And that's when I saw a transformation in my life. Words are powerful Nia. With effort and discipline, you have the power to eradicate excuses if you want to pay off your debt. Just because you can't do it today doesn't mean you can't do it tomorrow."

"You're living what you've been preaching to me." She clapped for him. "Okay! I see you Dad!"

"Quite frankly, if you want to make time for something, you'll make time for it, no matter how busy you are. I created a vision board for the rollout of this book and placed that quote on there as a constant reminder."

"*Quite frankly,*" Nia began, imitating him. "You're pulling out the author language on me already?" She giggled. "That book is changing you already I can see!"

"You're funny," he stated, mirroring her amusement. "The writing process was pretty much everything I've been telling you. I first took control of the spiritual phase by believing in God, myself, and believing it could be done. I then took control of the mental phase by creating my plan for writing, which included all my deadlines, a vision board for inspiration and reminder of my 'why,' and an outline of the entire chronological occurrence of the book before laying it on paper. Finally, I took control of the physical phase and just executed, which is what I'm doing right now. I performed all of this with effort, 190% that is, and self-discipline, predicated by the discipline I had shown forth already with the various phases. *That* is why it's deep."

"That's amazing Dad!"

"Thank you, I try. I also became a great father you recognize today through applied effort and discipline. I got used to your periods through effort and discipline, because those things...I don't know. I just wasn't prepared to have you at the time, and it was a real learning curve, but I'm glad I stuck with it and I didn't abandon you and become another statistic."

"Hey! Hey! TMI Dad!"

"Sorry! Well, it's your last day of fasting." He presented her with a dashing smile. "Wow! How do you feel kiddo?" He lightly patted her shoulder.

"Ow Dad! You've got to stay out of the gym!"

"Relax. That's just a little love tap!"

"No. But I feel great! I definitely think I evolved spiritually and mentally, but I'm just thinking, now what? I'm still scared of public speaking."

"And public speaking is an important one. Wherever you finish college, you're going to need that skill at one point. You already know my stance about minimizing your debt by spending your first few years at community college and transferring, but you have to prioritize what makes you happy. But, remember again, just because you can't do it today doesn't mean you can't do it tomorrow."

"Oh! That's one thing I've learned about myself during this journey. That growth mindset stuff is really true!"

"I go deeper into it in the book too. *The Power of Yet* is really going to be a game changer. I know it might not happen right away, but I firmly believe this manuscript is going to change the world or spark the brain that will."

"Okay Tupac."

"Man," he began grinning. "On a serious note, the book is about taking control of the spiritual, mental and physical battles through viewing them as different phases. It's about applying 190% effort and being disciplined and applying these two principles to each of the battles in what I lay out in the book as the Rule of Six. I got a question for you: what's your why?"

"Huh? For what?"

"*Why* do you want to not fear public speaking anymore?"

"Oh yeah! My 'why' for doing stuff! *The Alchemist* was incredible by the way! Well...um...I just don't want to be scared and pass out anymore and I think that's my personal legend."

"So you just told me you can't even identify your 'why' that's unique to you. It's really important to identify your 'why' for measuring your likelihood of success towards the journey. When I'm coaching clients about their finances, that's a question I ask them, just like I asked you earlier. My 'why' for why I wanted to get rid of my fear of public speaking was to serve as a success story for those that are scared. I went from nearly in special education classes for not speaking in class to now giving speeches and inspiring millions of people across the globe." His words carried more weight as he raised the inflection of his voice. "I don't want to hear anything can't be accomplished with effort and discipline! I'm living proof!"

"Wow! I think I'll work on finding my 'why' then."

"Yup. You need to apply your 'why' with effort and discipline if you want to achieve *any* measurable amount of success. *That's* the secret formula."

"That's it? That seems so simple. Why doesn't everyone do that if it's so simple?"

"It seems simple, but everyone needs a reminder. It's about constantly thinking that way. They don't tell you the lifestyle you have to live in order to make sure it's concrete and lives on forever. Many people are misguided and undecided, so you should consider yourself blessed. I'm giving you valuable knowledge and wisdom right now." He smirked savvily and tapped his temple repetitively with his index finger. "It's all part of the plan."

"Okay, that makes a lot of sense then."

"I have to keep repeating myself just in case you haven't grasped this concept yet. Part of the plan is maintaining the lifestyle I told you about *even after* you get over your fear, or accomplish anything you aim to achieve."

"So when I achieve success, keep living that lifestyle?"

"Exactly! When you attain any ounce of success, you want to *keep* doing what got you to that level of success in order to maintain it. Most people don't do that and quit putting forth the same energy when they initially achieve success. This is such a simple thing to do, but also easy to overlook. I'm going to recommend you read *The Slight Edge* by Jeff Olson. He discusses the concept of the Slight Edge, which is a framework for success. It's about this. It's like dieting once you get your ideal body. You'll go back to being overweight again if you ditch your plan that blessed you with success."

"Okay, that puts things into perspective a lot clearer."

"Speaking of dieting, part of the lifestyle is to exercise physically to maintain a respectable physical frame to mentally be able to construct logical decisions. It's about taking control of those physical battles. You already took control of the spiritual battle through prioritizing your relationship with God through fasting, so be consistent with effort and discipline in that avenue. Do that with effort and discipline!"

"You sound like a broken record Dad," Nia replied rolling her eyes.

"Like I told you, I'm going to repeat myself as much as necessary, because I really need to make sure you get this," he began smirking. "Through your thick, big headed skull."

"I got this head from you!"

"Touché."

It was nearing the end of the day and Nia returned to her room. She took time to reflect on her 21-day victory following her final prayer. In deep thought, she realized in a town where the two choices were black and white, she came to the conclusion her fasting journey was an avenue to exercise her choice of focus. She still had mental voices attempting to guide her away from a focused endeavor. She could easily be among the negative influences in her city like most inhabitants and possibly change her life for the worst, but her brother was a constant reminder of her focus. She had an epiphany.

"My 'why' is making sure Simba's life wasn't in vain while making an impact on other girls that look like me to confidently pursue not only Computer Science but other aspirations in technology. Wow!"

Nia had newfound hope in her future and creating an opportunity for herself and those that followed her. She desired to relocate to a new city and tell her story about her journey and the pivotal role Simba played in it. Consciously uncomfortable with public speaking, she knew she wanted to communicate her story one way or another. Identifying her 'why' electrocuted her with a jolt of certainty she rid herself of her fear of public speaking.

"I got it! I'm going to tell my story in my essay for my application and if UCLA accepts me I might tell it to others through public speaking." She cringed as the words left the tip of her tongue. "That sounds crazy out loud! But I think I can do this! Dad believes me! My future self believes me! Mom believes me! Simba believes me! And God believes me! Time to write that essay now that I know what I want to say!"

Nia hurried and retrieved her laptop. She decided to type outside, next to her balcony. She let the chilling wind of the night penetrate her pores, while she confided in her own world, staring at a bright screen surrounded by darkness. She thought deeply about her 'why' and how she would implement it in her story for her application. The computer loaded up while she retrieved her phone and immersed herself in the beat of Solange's "Almeda," vibrating like a ripple of aggressive fluidity while Solange tamed the beast that was the beat with her sweet voice, likened to a rose.

"It's all part of the plan I guess."

She looked up in the air, noticing the dark clouds as she fell in deep thought. She noticed how the stars coexisted gracefully with the night's surface, while reminiscing about her mother.

"Nia, a star can only shine in darkness."

"Wow! I actually started something and finished it. I took control of my mind and tuned out all the naysayers. I actually love my natural hair now! The mind *is* really powerful, and I took control of mine!" She grew emotional as she shed joyful tears that leaked on the 'F' and 'J' keys on her keyboard, traveling towards the 'D' and 'I' keys. "21 days? I think this is what Dad meant about the physical phase, because I'm actually about to do this application finally, with effort and discipline!"

MENTAL EXERCISES

WHAT'S YOUR RELATIONSHIP WITH MONEY?

In the mental phase, Nia is provided actionable steps her father implemented to pay off his student loan debt quickly. He reveals the GoldenOne Dream lifestyle and goes in depth of his process towards financial freedom.

The mental phase is controlled when you apply the power of planning using your mind.

*Upon reading this phase, I now ask you again: **what's your relationship with money? Write it down.** Take out an additional piece of paper and copy your answer onto the new sheet. Compare it with your other paper from the spiritual phase. Is there a difference? Why or why not? Fold this sheet of paper and carry it with you until you finish this book. Re-read the GoldenOne Dream lifestyle to acquire knowledge and wisdom towards financial freedom.*

_____

_____

_____

_____

_____

_____

_____

_____

_____

_____

_____

_____

_____

_____

_____

_____

_____

MEDITATION IS PERMANENT HEALING!

Nia's father describes the effectiveness of daily meditation. He distinguishes between those that self-medicate through medication versus those that meditate. I challenge you to implement meditation within your regimen. Create a plan to meditate daily.

The mental phase is controlled when you apply the power of planning using your mind. *If you are a beginner, start by focusing on meditating for one minute daily and build up to two minutes, three minutes, and so on. If you don't know how to meditate, one way is focusing on your breathing while taking deep, consistent inhales and exhales, focusing your thought solely on your breath. If you are still unsure, Google and YouTube are great resources.*

Try it right now. ***Meditate for five minutes. How do you feel? Write it down.*** *Meditation is an important tool towards debt freedom because it promotes the ability to make sound decisions. Re-read the GoldenOne Dream lifestyle to acquire knowledge and wisdom towards financial freedom.*

FOOD FOR THOUGHT

While describing the GoldenOne Dream lifestyle, Nia's father questions her reasoning for wanting to be free from student loan debt. It is important to know your 'why' for the purpose of making your pursuit stronger. As it pertains to student loans, I now ask you:

What's your why?

Why do you want to be student loan free?

Based on your money management as the CFO of your life, would you keep yourself employed today or fire yourself?

He also describes the fact that we can be quitters, campers or climbers. Most people are campers and the overall goal of this concept is to reach the top of the mountain, defined as one's purpose. This analogy is effective for a mental picture that can smoothen the perception of the journey since you can visually see the top of the mountain. In regard to your aspirations: **what's your mountain?**

The mental phase is controlled when you apply the power of planning using your mind. *Part of using the mind is creating a plan to acquire adequate rest. Sleep is king!* **How many hours of sleep did you receive last night?** *I encourage you to take out a sheet of paper and write down your answers and keep them until you reach the end of the book. Re-read the GoldenOne Dream lifestyle to acquire knowledge and wisdom towards financial freedom.*

To the misguided and undecided body

Whose trials and tribulations contribute to a lack of action,

This phase is especially for you

As you plant your seeds of execution and satisfaction.

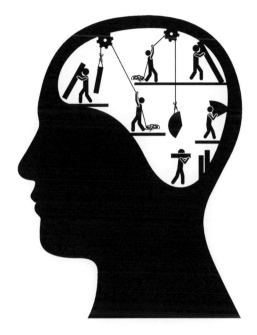

PART III

PHYSICAL PHASE

8

THE COMPOUND EFFECT IS DELAYED GRATIFICATION!

Nia rose from yet another victorious slumber, reflecting on the conquest of her fasting journey from a month ago. She had been working out consistently as directed by her father, ensuring she received a fair share of cardiovascular fitness and resistance training. She felt amazing. She was a climber and she climbed to the top of the mountain. She was ready to enjoy her day off from school and be pampered with compliments and love. She planned to do absolutely nothing again to reboot her entire entity because for the first time in her life she felt accomplished. She reflected on the fact she delivered a speech without passing out following her strenuous trials and tribulations. Although slight stuttering and heart palpitations persisted, she made noticeable progress with one of her greatest fears.

She had finished reading *The Slight Edge* like her father recommended. Counterintuitive to the lessons illustrated in the book, she didn't care how she moved forward with her goals. She recognized she was still a work in progress and simply desired rest and relaxation.

Nia felt free. She was released from the bondage of spiritual attackers. She was released from the mental prison she had been living in for so long. She even submitted her college appeal application for UCLA in her hope to get away from her local college. Equipped with the financial education her father provided her, she craved attending UCLA. She still desired attending partly for her brother's sake. She maintained awareness of her father's cry for the identification of her relationship with money. She remembered she made a promise with herself to rebuke money from taking control of her life to the point it killed her. Unconsciously adopting an abundance mindset with money, she agreed it was a superfluous resource she could always acquire, following the financial discussion with her father.

Nia attributed the fact she was finally able to get over the barrier of submitting her application being due to the fact she was able to take control of her spiritual, mental and physical phases like her father suggested. She was intentional about expressing her gratitude, traced back to their ritual of affirming Nia's worth. Life was going unexpectedly well for her.

There was still an underlying fear of success in the back of her mind sporadically. Realizing she had come so far, she knew it wouldn't be a feasible task to stay as relevant as she was on her next ventures. She would have to work extremely hard to be viewed successful from her eyes, because she had accomplished many admirable accomplishments thus far that made most successes following the former not as impressive. This thought imposed massive pressure on Nia's psyche as she redirected her thoughts elsewhere.

Despite this mental hiccup, it was not as strong as it had once been due to her recently adopted mental stimulations of exercising and meditation. Fear of success was still lingering in the back of her mind, but it was more of an afterthought, if anything. Predicated by her relationship with Simba, she had a slight bout of post-traumatic stress disorder with success. However, at this point in her life, she took control of this mental psychological struggle for the most part.

"Wow, I've really come far," Nia began, reflecting on her journey, accompanied with a chuckle. "I used to wonder what the point of fasting was, but I get it now. Dad talks about finances and all those other things and how it relates to the control of the three battles. What if there are more? Now I get why he didn't just talk about money right away. Everything I had to learn prior to the financial education built up to the financial literacy and what I know now. That guy's good."

Nia paused as she fell in deep thought. She realized she learned a very important lesson during her journey.

"Discipline held very true when it came to my experience with fasting. If I can control something as simple as how much I eat, and do it consistently with exerting a huge effort, I'm equipped with the tools to get rid of any debt I come across. So Dad must have fasted and that helped him be debt free super quick because he learned to be disciplined?" She paused briefly pondering her question. "I know for sure it helped him have a growth mindset as a result of that training he went through. I want it now though! I want to pay off my debt and be loan free right now! I want to be at UCLA now! I want to be completely comfortable with speaking and tell my story now!"

After reflecting a bit more, Nia left her room to participate in human interaction. She first went to her father's room and noticed he wasn't present. She traveled downstairs. Noticing his feet on the table crossed, the rest of his body was revealed as she made her way into the kitchen, noticing him with a newspaper in his hand, carefully analyzing it. He stumbled upon an interesting read as evidenced in his elicited facial expression. She attempted to capture his attention through clearing her throat obnoxiously and dropping random objects, but he didn't move an inch. She proceeded to play Chamillionaire's "Ridin'" on her phone, because the song made him move, but he still failed to budge and remained focused.

"Wow!"

"What Dad?"

"This kid got rid of his student loans in one year! $30,000!" He scanned the article and widened his eyeballs, reading a particular part that shifted his facial expression. "He did it at 23 years old! I'm going to meet this kid and have a conversation with him."

"Wow, that's great for that student!"

"He sounds like my long lost son!"

"Dad!"

"Just kidding sweetie! But he's pretty much saying he did it through the ways I'm telling you to have a growth mindset and take control of your finances. He might not know that's what he did, but that's what he did. Growth mindset is a universal law for success." He continued scanning the article and muttering to himself. "He's talking about delayed gratification. Interesting! That makes me forget! We should have focused on delayed gratification a *long* time ago. I wish we went over it well before you entered college, but better late than never."

"Okay, delayed gratification? It's just waiting for something right? Seems simple to me."

"No! Live like no one else, so you can live like no one else. *That's* what delayed gratification is about."

"Wow!"

"It's simple, but so many people *still* fail to execute this concept. It's very easy to just look at it and say it's simple. That's why there are so many kids with student loans. People will look at this newspaper and say it's simple that he just paid off his loans in one year by being disciplined in the same breath they're swimming in loans like they're training to compete with Michael Phelps. It's easy to see something done when you aren't the one doing it."

"That's true. I finished the book you told me to read by the way."

"Oh nice! How did you like it?"

"It was really good. I see what you were saying about success now."

He didn't seem sold.

"What did I mean about success?"

"You basically said how he talks about how you have to keep doing what made you successful *even after* you become successful to continue being successful."

He seemed elated. "Now that's a mouthful. Exactly! That's my smart baby girl! He made a point about how you have to master the mundane. Perseverance is a great substitute for talent, so you have no excuses not to succeed. I told you that day in the car your innate gift is discipline, because I'm familiar with your personality and I knew you didn't believe it. But I knew if I told you that you were disciplined, you would rise to the occasion upon my validation to make sure it stood true. *That's* your gift! You've got grit!"

"Wow Dad! You're so sneaky!"

"I'm just playing a game of chess for your development honey." He shrugged as he grew excited. "But Jeff Olson was telling you what I'm telling you. He was talking about having a growth mindset!"

"No he wasn't Dad," Nia replied dismissively, with a slight chuckle. "Any other good reads you think I should read though?"

"Since we're on this financial game topic, I want you to read *The Compound Effect* by Darren Hardy."

"Why?"

He pointed towards the newspaper entry he was discussing earlier. "This kid in here paid off his student loans quickly and he's talking about delayed gratification. That book gives you game on that. I'll be *damned* if my own seed isn't doing the same, if not better!" He rubbed his hands together, producing a sound indicating that they were ashy enough to ignite a fire. "I guess class is in session again."

"Oh God," she replied sulking, as he laughed profusely.

"These will be very valuable lessons like usual so don't fret. I want to start off with this motto I firmly use and live by, which is why we still have a roof over our heads, so I *must* be doing something right."

Nia scanned their luxurious residence. For Notsuoh, this was a palace to many and she quickly realized he had an irrefutable point.

"Listen! The motto is: Acquire money, keep money and use money. That's how you build generational wealth. I wish I was told this information early on. You're so lucky and blessed!"

"Okay Dad, I'm listening. Can you break that one down for me?"

"I would be honored," he bowed with a grin. "You remember my theory I told you earlier about humans?

"The fact we're a hunter-gatherer society and aren't wired to save?"

"Ex-actly!" He oscillated his index finger in an animated fashion like a host of a game show. "So just a reminder: saving money requires an override of our natural human conditioning and that's why it's so hard for people to pay off their debts and execute on the principle of delayed gratification, while appreciating the byproduct of compound interest that comes with it. That's my opinion though."

"Hmm, okay. That seems to make sense to me though."

"Good. So I want you to read that book, because you need to have a reason to want to participate in compound interest." He paused in a deep thought. "Okay, let me tell you about 401k."

"401k. 401,000?"

"No sweetie," he replied laughing. He appeared reluctant to continue speaking as if he was about to speak on a taboo topic. "I didn't want to tell you since it's early and I don't want to bore you since I know how you are, but it's for your benefit. I know you like talking about money, but it depends on how we talk about it and this tends to be the boring side of money. 401k is a retirement plan, not 401,000."

"Oh! No I want you to tell me. I'm different now. Is that for old people like you?"

"Ha-ha! Very funny."

"I'm just kidding," she replied coyly. "Does the 401k part at least come from 401,000?"

"Nope. 401k comes from section 401, subsection (k) of the IRS regulations. That has nothing to do with the amount of money in it."

"Oh okay!"

"So when you work full time, you're going to want to be aware of the fact your company has a 401k plan."

"I'm working full time? I thought I shouldn't be an employee. You work for yourself?"

"Yes, but working full time at first is a great stepping stone to see how other companies function as inspiration in your own ventures when you decide to start your own company. Not everyone does it the way I did it, but that was just my reality. You define your own reality. There's also nothing wrong with working a job if that makes you happy, but I just want you to be aware of the importance of having options because quite frankly, many of these companies will let you go without notice. Having an abundance mindset is the only way to win this game of work."

"Okay, I'll work to get experience and learn from the companies and apply it to my own businesses."

"Yes! Businesses! I love that pluralized wording! Anyway, I didn't have anyone tell me about a 401k plan so when my job gave me that big package of different plans employees could participate in, I just glanced at it and didn't think much of it. It wasn't until I had a mentor at my job that looked like me, old enough to be my father stop me and ask me if I was taking advantage of the 401k plan and benefits."

"You had a mentor too! Wow! What did you tell him?"

"I looked at him like he was crazy. I was young and no one could tell me anything at this time. I thought I knew it all. I was young and misguided. And you know what this man told me when he saw I was lost?"

"What?"

"He said, 'if you're misguided and undecided, knowledge and wisdom could be provided' and that really resonated with me. That's when I realized he had something special to say and I learned a lot of what I know about finances and growth mindset from him."

"Oh wow Dad! You never told me that was where you got it from! I remember Simba said that quote and wouldn't tell me what it meant. What does that quote mean?"

"Now you know where a lot of my knowledge comes from. That's why I told you about the importance of having a mentor. The quote actually speaks about the power of mentorship."

"How?"

"He said, 'If you're misguided and undecided, knowledge and wisdom can be provided.' This means you should be cognizant of the fact that someone has been through what you're going through. No matter what you want to accomplish in life, someone has experienced that before you and it's important to take advantage of this. There's power in knowing this, because most young people in the world are misguided and just need that guidance to motivate them and influence them to move forward correctly."

"Wow okay, and you're my mentor so it's all adding up."

"Yup! He's the one that put me onto *Mentor: The Kid & The CEO*. Look at Notsuoh and its inhabitants. One can be misguided, which means they aren't focused and can potentially be influenced by the wrong people and fail. Another individual can be on the cusp of failure and focus, which means they're undecided. For either of these individuals, knowledge and wisdom can be provided to transform their situation for the greater good."

"That really resonates with me Dad. I'll be honest, throughout my entire fasting journey and even now I feel like I'm an undecided individual and it's hard to get out of that mental prison. It's good to be aware of the fact that knowledge and wisdom can be provided and I think moving forward, that'll help me focus more and thrive."

"Trust me Nia, you might feel that from within, but you're definitely leaning more towards a path of focus. And you can follow both paths. We all have our demons and encounter many battles, but we must persevere and use our resources. Knowledge and wisdom can be provided to reset your mindset like that morning coffee a lot of people need in the morning.

"Knowledge is the information one gains over a period of time, so obviously some people have more knowledge than others. Wisdom is deeper and pretty much someone's ability to apply that knowledge and assess its validity. Knowledge is like acquiring a puzzle piece, whereas wisdom is *knowing where* to place the puzzle piece. That's why knowledge is potential power, rather than power. In order for that knowledge to be powerful, one must have the wisdom to utilize it correctly."

"I never really looked at the two and compared them, so I appreciate you making the distinction. I like the puzzle piece analogy. That makes a lot of sense."

"Yup. Anyway, you have to take advantage of your job's 401k plan and I'm going to tell you why."

"Why?"

"Patience. So it's important to take advantage of your 401k plan, because companies participate in a match, which is basically where they contribute a matching dollar amount to your retirement savings and it's basically free money. Don't leave free money on the table."

"Wow, why didn't you do it?"

"Because I knew it took money out of my paycheck and I wanted my money right away. I was in a fixed mindset plagued by instant gratification. My mentor taught me how to live in a growth mindset and appreciate delayed gratification, because it was saving today for a greater tomorrow. I didn't see it that way initially."

"Wow! I thought you were always in a growth mindset."

"Nope. My development was sparked by both your mother and my mentor. The thing was I was years in my career and nearly in my 30s before I grasped this concept, so I was obviously mad, but it was better late than never. I'm here to tell you: don't wait any longer! Embrace delayed gratification and take advantage of your 401k match. You'll thank yourself later!"

"Okay, but how does delayed gratification relate to compound interest?"

"You're ahead of me," he replied happily. "Great question! So your 401k plan accrues interest over time. Basically, compound interest means that it keeps earning interest or growth on the growth you've already earned over time."

"Do you have an example?"

"Yes. Let's say you have $2,000 in your 401k and it grows by 8%. You would end up with $2,160. If you earned just 8% on the same $2,000 in the second year, you'd get another $160, giving you $2,320, so your money is constantly working for you in your favor. Compound interest is king! I missed out on that for years! To catch up to someone that started before me I would have to contribute way more money out of my comfort zone and still not catch up to them, so the power of compound interest is unmatchable. Start now!"

"Okay wow! That's important to be conscious of. Now I see why you talk to a lot of students about these topics."

"Yes! I'm passionate about this, because no one prepared me for this stuff early on. I fully believe in these concepts and if I'm speaking about it throughout the world I need to make sure *you* fully understand it as well."

"Okay! I'm all ears! Is there anything else I should be worried about?"

"Well, not worried, just be prepared and you'll excel. You should also consider opening a Roth IRA account. That is a Roth Individual Retirement Account. I know I'm talking retirement, but I've given you the game to already get rid of your loans and any debt you accrue, so these are the next steps after you've reached financial freedom. I want to give you game to expand your horizon and build foundational wealth. That's a lacking thing in our community and a motivation for why I started the GoldenOne Dream concept."

"Sounds good. Let me hear about the Roth IRA thing."

"So a Roth IRA is a good savings option, because it allows your money to grow tax free. You're funding it in after-tax dollars."

"What does after-tax dollars mean?"

"That means you already paid taxes on the money, and is important, because with a lot of other retirement accounts, when you take out the money, you'll be paying a pretty hefty tax depending on how much you've got saved. I tell you this for the purpose of telling you the importance of having multiple bank accounts. It's important to diversify your funds, because you shouldn't put all your eggs in one basket. It's about having an abundance mindset!"

"I should have an abundance mindset. Got it."

"Yes! Having a growth mindset is about having an abundance mindset! That's what everything I'm telling you right now can be summed up to. That's why you need to diversify your funds. Just because someone knows how to do something one way, doesn't mean you should only be focused on their way. You can be aware of their way, but also create your own way."

"I'm a leader, not a follower Dad!"

"You read a few books and now you think you're big time huh?" He inquired laughing. "But you've got to remember you have the opportunity most people don't have. Most people your age aren't aware of what I'm telling you. Many people that are older than you aren't even equipped with the necessary financial mindset I've bestowed upon you. Now it's up to you if you are going to focus and reap the fruits of your labor, or fumble the opportunity like you're average and fail."

Nia felt his words in her soul. Knowing her circumstantial advantage and history with her brother veering off his path, she didn't want to disappoint her father. She desired to make sure his work wasn't accomplished in vain. Knowing she took control of her spirituality and mentality, she now had to focus on mastering arguably the most important aspect: physicality. Executing was the golden ticket for the VIP entrance leading towards the gate of success away from general admission of those that failed to execute.

"Compound interest is delayed gratification, Nia. Go ahead and read that book and you'll see for yourself. The power of starting early is undefeated. I'm going to put that in my book. I'll illustrate saying, 'if you're reading this you're probably relatively young' and I say that, because I want to make it a point to my audience whether you deem yourself young or not, your age is younger than your age plus one so that's still starting early. Start now!"

"That's an interesting concept on its own too. There's always someone older that can make you feel young too."

"Shoot! If you want to talk about old people, old people are important, because they allow us to see the future." Nia quickly pondered about her spiritual encounters with her failed-future self. "Most people forget to save for retirement and we see the detriment of that in those that come before us."

"I really believe in that Dad! I'm so glad you're telling me all this, and I appreciate all of the conversations we have even though we tend to clash a lot."

"Aww sweetie, I appreciate you too." He kept his composure of being a teacher. "But like I said, delayed gratification is sacrificing *today* for a greater tomorrow. You can't cram the night before a test and hope it'll work in your favor. You've got to put in the work *early* and enjoy the compounded knowledge. Don't have a fear of losing money, you'll make it back."

"Why do you say that about losing money?"

"Remember my philosophy: acquire money, keep money, and use money. You *have* to *use* money to make more money. It may sound counterintuitive, but that's progressive and how I and many others have not only built a foundation for generational wealth, but had the guts to get rid of our debt quickly. Don't be afraid to lose it all, because you should have an abundance mindset relationship with money."

"Oh yeah! You did say that earlier about knowing your relationship with money and how it's abundant so we shouldn't be afraid to lose it all. Noted."

"Yes, I'll refresh your memory. A lot of people are broke, because they clutch their money like it's their last and they don't have the tools necessary to produce more money. They don't have the favorable mindset. If you look at money like it's a finite resource in your life, you'll live in a fixed mindset and never grow. Most people don't invest in themselves. As soon as I finish my book, there will be people asking for it for free and asking for discounts. They don't see the value in investing in their future, but my readers will!

"When you bet on yourself and invest in yourself, you're spending money, because you know in the long run, the information you gain access to will pay forward your initial investment exceedingly. Have an abundance mindset! Take risks and don't be afraid to lose it all, because you have the knowledge base to know it'll come back eventually. That's delayed gratification! That's the mindset you need to understand to pay off your student loans quickly!"

"That's so true about people not investing in themselves. Now I see why you say it's about sacrificing today for a greater tomorrow. A lot of people aren't willing to do that."

"Most people, but exactly! I'm a risk taker. I'm not afraid to lose it all. I know I can get more, so I'm equipped with the mindset to always be surrounded by money!

"Also, one of the most important things my mentor told me about all of these financial drawbacks I was experiencing was that when you learn information you need to pass it on to the next generation. It's a perpetual cycle. So you know what that means?"

"I'll pass the information you're giving me to the next person."

He nodded and smiled proudly, opening the fridge to retrieve a fresh apple.

"All this information," he began as he took an aggressive bite. "It's really important, because it's a sense of urgency since I wish someone warned me earlier years ago when I had no money saved. I paid off my student loans early, but even with that, you're learning this as a freshman in college. I was years in my career barely figuring this out. You'll definitely thank me later when you're flourishing in riches."

"I *definitely* will. I used to not understand why I should listen to what you had to say, but I think it's clearer now."

"And don't just listen to me though. Execution is the divisive factor between those that succeed and those that fail. Remember they are very similar, so you might as well succeed. Listen! Success and failure are very similar so you might as well strive to succeed."

"Okay, will do Dad! That's a great point, because I read somewhere, I think it comes from Thomas Edison, and he said, 'a dream without execution is hallucination' which I found powerful."

"Wow! That is powerful! I haven't heard that one, but that's amazing. You see? I learn from you as well. But like he said, execute!"

"How do you execute though? I feel like it's easy to say execute and do this, that, and the third, but I just think it's hard to actually do it."

"Reframe your mind to know that execution is a physical battle within your mind and spirit. When you take control of your mind first, it'll make execution easier. Amongst spiritual, mental and physical battles, physical battles are the most straightforward and should be easiest to take control of, because you're simply doing.

"Okay, I'm going to ask you a question right now and I don't want you to play with me. You like food right?"

"Yes? I don't see where this is going though."

"Having a growth mindset is about the fact that we must remember to E.A.T."

"Eat what?"

"E.A.T. is an acronym for 'execute and thrive.' I'm not talking about lobster, steak and shrimp. We might have to get that after this conversation though. But, you also have to make sure you eat physically too, because you need the energy from food to E.A.T., execute and thrive! When you *do*, you'll *succeed!*"

"That's a cool acronym!"

"Yeah, it's what I tell my audience. I lead a chant where I yell, 'Let' E.A.T.!' and they love it! The concept of E.A.T. is one of my favorite concepts because it's essentially what allows you to take control of the physical phase and overcome physical battles you come across. That's probably the knowledge base you need most at this point in time it seems."

"Yeah, but how does that relate to my life?"

"Okay," he began as he pulled out his phone. "I'm going to show you one painting and I want you to rate it on a scale of one through ten and you can't use seven."

"Why not?"

"Just follow my exercise dear."

He pulled up an image of the painting while Nia feasted her eyes on it meticulously. It was an abstract painting of a lion appearing to chase a gazelle. In her mind, it was great, but at the same time it wasn't so great. Staring at it for quite some time, she pondered the score she would give it, whilst contemplating if her father's activity had a relevant point. He interrupted her lengthy train of thought, spanning from New York to California.

"You see how you haven't made a decision? I instructed you *not* to use seven in your rating, because I'm forcing you to make a decision. I put you in the position to have to make a decision, because six is a score that's barely passing and eight is a score that's above passing. Seven is a score that's in the middle, and it's the safest answer anyone can come up with. You have to execute under all conditions! 99% of people think aimlessly, 1% do! When you *do*, you'll *succeed!*"

"I see why you're getting paid for speaking engagements now Dad. That's a genius idea! I knew in my head I would have said seven if you didn't steal it from me, because it looked good, then it looked not as good."

"I know. But you see how you haven't passed out from speaking ever since that day too? You've continually been E.A.T.ing over time and you're obviously still nervous but you're better. That's also related to the compound interest topic, because your effort and consistency with speaking has compounded, making you better over time. And that's related to delayed gratification, because you've made those notable sacrifices to continue pushing forward instead of quitting and assuming your speaking skills wouldn't ever improve. Compound interest is delayed gratification! A byproduct of that is having a growth mindset."

"It's crazy how everything you're saying works in a cyclical way." She grabbed her head out of confusion. "You really know what you're talking about sometimes. That's crazy."

"Sometimes?" He inquired as if he had been disrespected.

"I'm joking Dad," she replied giggling. "You should see your face! Is compound interest ever bad?"

"Yes! I'm glad you asked, because it's about perspective. Like many things, when in the hands of a particular party, we can view it as positive or negative. Compound interest is obviously bad when you look at things like student loans and the culture we have today where kids and parents alike think it's acceptable to pay them off forever, when it's not! They embrace the concept of borrowing early, but not returning it early. They borrow early and over the years of paying their minimum payment, they don't see a change, because it keeps accruing and compounding. They need to take a risk and stop paying simply the average amount!"

"Dang, I felt like you were attacking me with that," Nia began, as they both chuckled. "I didn't even think about that. They really give us the opportunity to take out loans early and get ourselves in a rut."

"Yup. *That's* the type of starting early that's detrimental if you don't keep the same energy on the other end and pay it off early. Our culture preaches half the story, when there's an entire other side of the story or equation that isn't being acknowledged. You take them out early, so pay them off early as well. I only recommend that if it's convenient at least. Every situation is different. The most important part is having the mindset to understand this phenomenon. Everything starts with the mind Nia."

"You keep saying everything starts with the mind. But I think I get it now. Compound interest is bad when you don't think about the fact your student loan balance or debt is compounding interest to where you'll pay more than you started with?"

"Exactly!"

"And it's good when it works in your favor to multiply your retirement money or any investment that generates money?"

"You're on fire."

"Hmm," Nia got excited from the validation from her father and thought of some additional information to add. "And the bad compounded interest isn't delayed gratification, because they aren't sacrificing for a greater tomorrow?"

"Yeah," her father chuckled. "That's more like delayed freedom!"

"I like that, because we want financial freedom. We have the ability to be free, but we aren't free since it's delayed."

"Yeah, not *yet*. We're on the same wavelength sweetie!" His energy shifted, grabbing Nia as she observed a sense of urgency in his eyes. "Do you promise me to execute and live out what I've taught you today?"

"Yes! Let's E.A.T.!" She replied without skipping a beat.

9

THE POWER
OF YET MEANS

Many months had passed by. Nia made her best effort to live the GoldenOne Dream lifestyle granted to her, but inevitably had to get acclimated to it from time to time.

Nia found herself enrolled at UCLA as a Computer Science major. She graced the campus confidently, dismissing her initial compelling preconceived notions she would be judged for her choice in a technological field. Glancing around aimlessly, she felt ecstatic at the fact everyone appeared extremely happy in blue and gold. The clean ambience of the campus was a blissful experience that sold her instantly. As their tour stopped briefly, she took a moment to retrieve coffee on the campus; her choice of drink was a caramel mocha. She didn't drink coffee, but the atmosphere of the campus influenced her to push the boundaries of what she typically endured.

"This school is already changing me," she whispered to herself in between sips of her beverage.

She glanced down at her shirt as a drip of coffee met the "C" on the UCLA shirt she sported as she grew slightly frustrated. She quickly smeared it with her fingers and returned back to her group. As they roamed the campus on their way to the library, they observed its radiant sun shining brightly whilst being comforted by a chilling wind. Everything was perfectly aligned how it was supposed to be.

"All my hard work really paid off. I submitted that appeal and I got in as a Computer Science major! A black girl? Wow!"

Nia was a female, black Computer Science student infiltrating the space of a campus that marginalized people that looked like her. She finished her beverage, and in the blink of an eye, found herself in the library studying for a test diligently. She found herself frustrated as she attempted to complete her assignment, failing repetitively. Her code wouldn't run correctly.

Glancing towards her classmates at the round table, they grew defensive and hid their laptop screens before her lips separated to ask a genuine question for assistance. She began to feel out of place, but convinced herself this was still what she wanted. She rose up confidently, making her way to the appropriate office hours in her attempt to diagnose the issue she couldn't solve.

When she arrived, she noticed her professor appeared as if she didn't want to be there. Removing her fingers from her phone and glaring at Nia as she stepped in the empty room, she crossed her arms. Nia felt uncomfortable, but set her laptop down on the professor's desk and mustered up the confidence to ask how she was doing.

"I'm okay. What do you need?"

"Um. I need help solving this code. I don't know why it won't run."

"Honey, you're not meant to be at this school."

"What?"

"*Your kind* isn't welcomed at this institution of academic excellence."

"Excuse me?"

Nia heard a new voice.

"Nia! Wake up!" It was a voice closer to her as she felt an unexpected nudge to her shoulder. "We're here at UCLA!"

Nia quickly woke up aggressively as saliva dripped from her mouth, streaming toward her chin.

It was all a dream.

She was still welcome on campus as far as she was concerned. She now remembered she was on a bus on the way to UCLA. She consistently had dreams of attending UCLA and representing the life Simba didn't get the chance to experience.

Nia was now on campus. Everything was now real and tangible. She quickly got off and attended the tour as they discussed topics concerning enrolled students.

As the tour ended, she isolated herself by making her way to the bathroom. She found a mirror, captured an analysis of herself, and the reality set in. She gazed at the letters on her sweater that didn't read those letters she worshiped: UCLA. Returning outside, she witnessed the letters scattered around the campus: UCLA. It was like she couldn't glance in any direction without seeing those traumatic letters that had traumatized her for so long. She learned to be grateful with the fact she wasn't accepted or denied into UCLA through her appeal application since her father helped grow her mindset, but in the back of her mind she was still human and felt slightly disheartened. Despite that, she still had hope she could get accepted, because they didn't deny her.

Nia reflected on her growth within the past year. With the lack of recurring dreams of visits from her failed future-self, her future seemed bright from her perspective. She wondered if she diminished her failed future-self to a memory because she had transcended towards her future successful self. She hoped for the best, but also maintained in her mind the possibility her failed future-self may have quit visiting her solely because she gave up on her. That thought was daunting. Nonetheless, her prioritized view was that she was on the path to be successful as long as she continued following through with her current mindset.

Walking around the campus once more with her collective, they began approaching a homeless man. They passed by him and held their noses as they stared at him, but Nia stopped abruptly after feeling a burning desire to give. She remembered her father coached her about giving as she read the sign he held up, insinuating he needed change. Sporting a new backpack and no longer ashamed to reveal it, she turned it facing the man as she rummaged through it for change.

It was pink with the letters 'GOD' in gold engraved in the back given to her by her father as an inclusion of his company's merchandise. It reeked of fresh material, equipping the user with the desire to wear it and succeed by any means. Her father granted her the opportunity to get rid of her old, dusty backpack so she felt compelled to give back. Stumbling across a couple crumpled up dollars she smiled and handed it to the man, as he accepted it while reciprocating her smile.

"God bless you sir!"

"God bless *you*! Everyone walked away from me and you were the only one that stopped. Why is that?"

"Um," Nia began replying as she didn't anticipate additional conversation. "I guess I just care...about humanity?"

"Yes, I can tell! Have you founded a company and call yourself the CEO of it?"

"No, but my Dad has. Why do you ask?"

"I see your backpack has a different look to it. I've also noticed in our society, many are compelled to call themselves the CEO of their company. They'll be like, 'I'm the CEO of this, I'm the CEO of that' and they don't even show they care about the company or the people they serve."

"That's interesting and true," Nia replied with a nervous giggle.

She didn't expect to gain knowledge from a homeless man.

"Yeah. I do a lot of thinking and reading, because I have time. CEO is a sexy term to use, but no one cares anymore. 'I'm the CEO of this company, I'm the CEO of that company' and it makes me think: has anyone ever thought about being the CCO? Chief Caring Officer!" Saliva flew from his mouth as he grew passionate.

"Oh my gosh," Nia replied in amazement, stealthily sidestepping from his saliva. "That's so true! I never thought about it like that sir."

"When you show people you care, you'll go far. I can tell you have a bright future ahead of you, because you're unconsciously displaying that altruistic characteristic just based off of our encounter. The CCO is arguably the most important person to any organization and it can be anyone in the organization. It can be the janitor and he or she will be more important to the organization than the ego booster that proudly calls him or herself the CEO."

"I'm actually so grateful that I came across you and was able to learn that sir. Please, is there anything else on the topic you could tell me?"

"Good companies have CEOs, great companies have CCOs!"

Nia evaded more saliva as he walked away gracefully. Despite dodging saliva a couple times, she felt a spiritual bliss travel throughout her body as a result of the encounter. What was formerly an old decrepit homeless man was now a seemingly wise man planting seeds of knowledge for the youth with exuberance. That simple encounter not only made his day, but it made her day, because she showed she cared and it showed.

A simple act of giving a couple dollars to a homeless man in need helped her just as much as it helped him. She pondered the possibility he hadn't smiled in quite some time prior to their encounter. Not only that, she realized once more her father was accurate about the concept of giving as it pertained to the GoldenOne Dream. The law of attraction was alive and well.

"If you're misguided and undecided, knowledge and wisdom can be provided," she thought to herself.

Reflecting on her current community college while roaming UCLA's campus, she agreed she would continue to reside in a boring space where she had those two options: focus or fail. She made her decision despite her circumstantial displacement that still made it unclear. Focus would be her intended path.

Stepping aside from the crowd she was with, Nia decided to give her father a phone call. She remembered how he preached the importance of checking in with loved ones, especially since he wouldn't be there with her forever in the physical form.

"Daddy?"

"Hey sweetheart," he replied in a deeper voice than usual, indicating he had just woke up from an afternoon slumber.

"I was talking to a homeless man right now and I gave him some money and it's crazy how the power of giving works like you told me!"

"Yes ma'am, it is alive and well." He cleared his throat. "What happened?"

"He was just telling me about how people should strive to be CCOs or Chief Caring Officers instead of CEOs since CCOs are the most important person in the organization, because importance comes down to caring."

"Now *that* is a message! I fully agree, but never formulated the words that way."

"Yeah! I was surprised. And he said good companies have CEOs, while great companies have CCOs."

"Wow! That reminds me, I want you to read *Good to Great* by Jim Collins at your time. Even if you don't read it right away, keep it on your list. You said you want to start a business eventually, so that's an amazing read to help give you the mindset I had when I started GoldenOne Dream. It'll help you guide those women looking to grace the tech. field. Was that why you called me though?"

"Okay, I'll put it on my list." Nia grew offended. "Dang! You act like I'm a terrible daughter! I was just calling to check in with you! UCLA hasn't denied my application so I still have hope, but they haven't given me an acceptance so I don't know. I guess I just wanted to check in with you since you always talk about doing that."

"Oh wow! That's so kind of you to listen to me," he stated, laughing playfully. "Honey, I just want to say I'm so proud of you and the progress you've made ever since you completed your fasting journey. Not only that, but you tuned out the negative demons in your head by taking control of your mental processes and learned to initiate action and be a true climber. You've excelled beyond measure and shown you're capable of having a growth mindset."

"You think so?"

"I think so. I think with your growth mindset, it can obviously still be expanded upon, but it's important to know that having a growth mindset is about The Power of Yet."

"Did you finish writing your book?"

"Not quite, but basically there. If you don't learn anything else from me I need you to remember that having a growth mindset *is* about The Power of Yet."

"Noted."

"The Power of *Yet* is what will allow you to know the difference between a growth mindset and a fixed mindset. Remember it darling?"

"Growth mindset person knows who they are, while a fixed mindset person doesn't know who they are."

"Excellent! The Power of *Yet* is what will allow you to realize you need to maximize your insecurities! The Power of *Yet* is what will allow you to understand the importance of having an abundance mindset. The Power of *Yet* is what will allow you to know that you need to *focus* on being intentional about having a high adversity quotient. You can be a quitter, camper or climber, but you want to be a climber and climb up to that mountain!"

"The Power of Yet is my idea though Dad. You basically plagiarized my idea from my dream!"

"Anyway, The Power of *Yet* is what will allow you to know we need to take control of those physical, mental and spiritual battles. The Power of Yet means you're taking control of your life. This is a battle of control! Take control and give yourself the life *you want* to live, not the one that was given to you by default."

"Okay Dad, I will."

"The Power of *Yet* is the golden rule to remember and you'll always have a growth mindset. That *yet* emits burning passion to succeed. It is with a burning desire to succeed that one is granted the opportunity to fully comprehend and acquire the vehicle towards liberation, The Power of Yet. It's with applied diligence, commitment and concerted effort one can break free from the shackles placed on the mind!

"It's with a burning desire that The Power of Yet means the power of belief! That *yet* is the belief you'll break through and be successful and become that Computer Scientist to inspire millions. That *yet* is the belief you'll pay off your debts! That *yet* is the foundation for believing, planning and executing towards a growth mindset and living the GoldenOne Dream. The Power of Yet means the power of God!

"You told me, 'I can't' several times when you fainted. Don't say that again! If you're going to say that, say 'I can't...yet' as a substitute. That *yet* is so powerful it can turn your dreams into reality! Whether you get into UCLA or not sweetie, I'm proud of you and your accomplishments, so make the best of your situation. You're a winner in my eyes."

"I didn't get into UCLA...*yet*." Nia grew emotional. "Thanks for all the support,

Dad. That makes me feel better. This conversation is actually worth more than a UCLA acceptance."

Nia confidently viewed the UCLA decision differently. She embraced The Power of Yet as she got off the phone with her father.

The same classmate that woke Nia up earlier from her deceiving slumber rushed over to her, questioning her ableness as she observed Nia taking deep breaths in between sniffs.

"Nothing," Nia replied, sniffing profusely. "I just had a life changing conversation and now know the meaning behind The Power of Yet."

"The power of...yet?"

Nia ignored her question and ran past her to the bathroom. "Fixed mindset people," she stated dismissively.

She arrived in front of the bathroom, stopping herself in her tracks aggressively to avoid colliding with the door and creasing her white sneakers.

Finding a mirror, she gazed at herself once more, inhaling and exhaling deeply as she began communicating with herself.

"*You...*yes! *You!* You're worthy of success! You have a loving father that'll always nurture you so you don't need no stupid UCLA to validate that! The name of a campus isn't going to hold you back, and besides that, they look at you as a check anyway." She clapped her hands against her cheeks aggressively. "Wake up Nia! The Power of Yet means taking control of your life! Taking control of those spiritual, mental and physical battles you were able to do and grant yourself the life you deserve to live!"

She stood in place as she continued to stare at herself, face to face with the perpetrator of her success. She now understood how her failed future-self didn't succeed. She took control of the spiritual and mental phases, but didn't take control of the physical phase. She didn't execute. Nia was further along than her failed future-self and content with this epiphany. Reminiscing about flipping through the final pages of *The Compound Effect* reminded her how she transcended into an executory mentality. People spend so much time on the other phases and being stagnant without taking consideration of the physical phase of execution. It's as simple as Nike stated it. It shouldn't require second thoughts, because execution is self-explanatory.

The Power of Yet meant taking control of one's life through each of the three battles. If any phase wasn't accounted for, it could be accounted for in the future, but it still had to be accounted for before victory. That was the power of that yet, the golden rule. Although this was a powerful rule, most people didn't embrace it. Most people choose to be a passenger, allowing their life to take control of them, rather than being the driver and taking control. Nia finally understood this concept. Nia sat confidently in the driver seat of her life.

"I'm Nia Akintewe and my father loves me! I deserve all the love in the world! The three pillars for financial success to get rid of my student loan debt or overcome anything I encounter is believing, planning and executing! Patience grants me the opportunity to take risks without consequences, because it gives me the mindset to focus on the fact I have time on my side. You can't be great without being grateful, and I'm grateful for everything.

"Actually, UCLA isn't stupid," she replied shyly. "I guess I was just mad. Just because I didn't get into UCLA, yet, doesn't mean I can't get in eventually. That's what a growth mindset is, and that's what The Power of Yet is!

I went from fainting from attempting to give speeches to now being able to give speeches consciously. I'm still very nervous, but I'm a work in progress and that's the power of that yet. I went through a 21-day fasting journey and developed my spiritual power beyond measure. *That's* The Power of Yet. I can always keep improving and take control of my spirituality. I've been given the mentality to pay off my student loans quickly and have the knowledge base to take on any mental struggle I come across. *That's* The Power of Yet. I've come along further than my failed future version of myself by understanding the importance of the physical phase, which is probably the most important phase that separates average from outlier. It separates camper from climber. Execution! *That's* The Power of Yet.

The Power of Yet is what will allow me to go to the next level! The Power of Yet means the power of belief! The Power of Yet means the power of planning! If you fail to plan, you plan to fail. The Power of Yet means the power of execution! The Power of Yet means the power of God! Amen!"

"Wow! That's impressive!"

Nia's armpits grew itchy as she glanced back in shock as someone joined her in the bathroom, listening in on her dialogue to herself. Laying her eyes on the unwelcome visitor, Nia observed a shy feeble looking girl that resembled herself prior to her comprehension of The Power of Yet.

As Nia laid her dilated pupils on her, another girl wearing expensive glossy headphones made her presence known. She walked past them gracefully playing her music at deafening levels as all in the bathroom heard Isaiah Rashad's "Heavenly Father." He rapped, "Just need a moment of silence" and she changed it to Solange's "Stay Flo."

Nia desired her moment of silence. She resonated with the girl's choice of music and imagined she would be friends with the girl if they crossed paths in a more appropriate setting. More importantly, she realized her time to reflect was ruined as students entered the bathroom sporadically. Her time of solitude came to an end.

"You should give speeches! The power of..yet? Can you enlighten me more on that? I want to hear more about your story and how you got to where you're at now...if you don't mind."

"I can."

10

I CAN!

Nia's UCLA application hadn't been denied nor approved yet, and it made her stomach turn like an indecisive rollercoaster, rarely maintaining a level path. It was the last day to hear a decision.

Today was the day.

Weeks had commenced since her tirade in the bathroom. Ever since that day when she enlightened the girl that disrupted her speech, countless people asked about her story. It was an unexpected domino effect.

Successfully transcending from a fixed mindset to a growth mindset was an admirable feat. Nia didn't view it as such, but she recollected her father's spiel about talents. People that possess a talent often downplay it, not observing the value others see in it, because it comes so naturally to them.

Nia's father rushed in her direction, embracing her gracefully. She heard music familiar to her ears playing loudly from the television as they simultaneously directed their vision its way. Elated, Nia's father nodded his head to the beat. Confused, Nia stared at the screen while scrunching her face like she smelled a foul odor.

It was "June 27th Freestyle" by DJ Screw.

"Dad, isn't this Drake's song?"

"You're so young," he replied with a disappointed sigh as he performed a face palm. "This is DJ Screw's song. He's a legend from Houston! Drake paid homage to him! You better put respect on his name! That's why Drake mentioned him in the beginning of the song, because *he's* paying homage. You youngsters man."

"Oh wow! *That's* DJ Screw! I thought this was Drake's song. My bad."

"Anyway, today's the day kiddo! You excited?"

"I'm just ready to hear a decision," Nia replied nonchalantly, shrugging. "I've done the work, now it's just a matter of keeping my faith in God. He'll provide the best for me no matter what happens. I'm already aware of my actionable plan to move forward no matter what the decision is."

"Nia. You've really evolved right before my eyes. I never knew when I would see you carrying yourself so effortlessly, operating in a growth mindset. I had faith you would get there and knew you were special, but you've evolved so quickly. It makes me so proud!"

"Well...now that you're happy, I think it's time I make a confession Dad."

"Shoot."

"I have a boyfriend now!"

His face grew serious.

"You have a what?"

Nia laughed obnoxiously.

"I see you're still in a fixed mindset with that though!"

"No no no. There's nothing wrong with you having a boyfriend anymore and I've come to terms with the fact it'll happen." He smiled deceivingly. "You just threw me off and I thought I was going to have to do something is all."

"No Dad," Nia replied as her heart raced. Losing track of time, she now realized it was time to log into her computer and view the acceptance or rejection. "It's time Dad!"

She retrieved her laptop and booted it up as her fingers trembled, her palms growing sweaty. This was the moment she had been waiting for. The moment she weighed so heavily by assuming this was the only avenue where she could honor Simba's life. She was about to witness the power of her application. She genuinely felt confident about her essay, detailing her unique story of transforming from a fixed mindset to a growth mindset; she went from fainting and failing to focus and fascination. Many loved hearing her story of overcoming, so why wouldn't UCLA take a fascination to it as well?

Attempting to log in was an immediate failure. She butchered the keys, while forgetting her password. Experiencing this brain fart, she began hallucinating extra letters along her keyboard as a result of a lack of sleep. Her body had endured spiritual, mental and physical blows throughout her tough journey of becoming a gatekeeper of The Power of Yet.

"Why don't you just get some rest? We can take a look at it later if you don't remember your information right now?"

"No! I'm just hungry."

She rose up from where she sat and retrieved a red, shiny apple. Aggressively chomping on it, she paced back and forth in the kitchen without a regard for her father's presence. She grew aware of the possible disappointment upon the decision looming the area. Chomping away at the apple, she nearly reached its core while widening the gap between her two front teeth in the process.

Suddenly, she stumbled upon an epiphany. She attempted to toss the half-finished apple in the nearby trash can, as it grazed the rim and met the ground's surface. Her father laughed.

"We have to work on your jump shot!"

She picked it up and placed it in the trash can successfully.

"I missed on purpose to give myself an extra opportunity!" She tapped her temple with her index finger. "That's growth mindset! I missed the first time, because I didn't make it, yet. The Power of Yet."

"Touché little one. Touché."

She placed her hands at her hips. "I'm not little!" She quickly changed her mood into a happy go lucky one. "But I remember my password!"

She ran over to the computer as her body digested the seed of knowledge and she successfully logged in. Her father glanced over at her as she stared at the screen. He nervously began making his way over to hover over her.

"So what did they say?"

Nia scanned the page aimlessly as she began experiencing bouts of blurred vision and nearly lost her ability to read as her vision cleared up.

"They rejected me."

"Oh wow. Sorry to hear that sweetie."

"It's fine. This decision doesn't define me."

"You're right. Are you finished with pursuing the Computer Science degree?"

"I can be done. But no, not yet. Those girls that look like me need me. I still have to do it. I can, and I will. Besides, this isn't the only way to honor Simba's life. I've come to terms with that at least, so I'm grateful for whatever blessing in disguise this situation is."

"I agree with you. I'm sure he would want you to live your life without placing all this insurmountable amount of pressure on yourself. You've got to be aware of your mental health as well. And wherever your brother is right now, I'm sure he's watching over you and wishes the best for you." Her father squinted as he scanned the bottom of the page. "What's that part about June 19th down there?"

"Huh?" She glanced back, looking up at her father. "It's not June 19th yet."

Nia scanned the page in search for the date her father mentioned. After meandering the page and speed reading, she laid her eyes on it.

"Oh! I see what you're saying now. It says, 'Although we are unable to grant you admission to UCLA's class for this term, many of our staff was touched by your essay! We want to extend an offer to you to be a speaker at UCLA's Juneteenth celebration on June 19th. This year's theme is mindfulness and focuses on overcoming mental battles. Growth mindset and The Power of Yet are very powerful topics and we would love to hear more about your story! We think you are the most suitable candidate for this opportunity and we would be honored to have you speak at our event. Monetary compensation will be discussed upon receipt of your decision.' That's how they feel. It's an opportunity so I guess I'll take it?"

"Wow!" Her father smiled as if he was alerted he won the lottery. "This is definitely an opportunity to expand your network! Congratulations! I personally think this is even better than an acceptance to attend their institution, because people *pay* to attend UCLA, but you're *getting paid* to attend UCLA!"

"I couldn't agree more Dad!"

"Are you familiar with Juneteenth, Nia?"

"I've heard of it being talked about, but not really. Can you tell me more about it?"

"You're in Texas and aren't familiar? I've failed!"

"Come on Dad!"

"I'm just kidding sweetie. It's not only a very important date, but very important to Black History that's been erased over time, because a lot of people outside Texas just aren't familiar with the history. Also, there hasn't been a priority about it since it isn't an officially celebrated national holiday. It's only a state holiday in certain states."

"Okay I see, but what's the real history behind it and all the other interesting stuff I should know about it?"

"Juneteenth is when Texas essentially acquired their freedom from slavery on June 19th, 1865. Texas wasn't at the center of the theatre of battle of the Civil War. There was a major general, Gordon Granger who arrived in Texas on June 18th and declared the emancipation of African-Americans the next day on June 19th, which became Juneteenth and if you didn't notice by now, the wording is a combination of June and nineteenth. Part of why it became nationally recognized is because of The Poor People's March in 1968."

"Wow! That's amazing and I didn't even know all of that. I knew the day was a thing, but didn't know it was that deeply rooted culturally and historically."

"Now you know. And you'd better know, because you've got a gig to kill during this year's Juneteenth!"

"I'll definitely do more research now that I received this opportunity. Wow, I'm so thankful for all of this. I never thought I would say it, but I'm so glad UCLA rejected me!"

"First of all, you *earned* this opportunity. But a blessing in disguise is what I call that!"

"Honestly. And the funny thing about you telling me this is I thought about something for my speaking engagement." Nia blinked her eyes rapidly attempting to fight back the tears from breaking through. "Wow! That seems crazy just to even say I'm doing speaking engagements now."

"The mind. It's a very powerful thing, Nia. Remember, it can play tricks on you. But what were you thinking?"

"I mean this with respect. Not only was Juneteenth an abolition to slavery, but it's an abolition to my old habits and chains tied around my mind I once had when I was living life in a fixed mindset. I broke from those chains leaving the dark depths of depressive thoughts, feeling like I wouldn't amount to anything and now I celebrate having a growth mindset.

"I've conquered most of my fears and insecurities. I've passed my written driving test and the behind the wheel test, clocking in many hours of drive time. I've been doing speeches without passing out. I no longer say I'm bored and recognize that can be detrimental to one's focus not only as a resident in Notsuoh, but towards anything someone wishes to get in life. That's my Juneteenth and what it means to me now. And then I'll ask them all to identify their own Juneteenth. How does that sound Dad?"

"Bingo! You're already a speaker!"

"Thanks Dad! All because of God, you, and all my loved ones watching me from above wherever they are."

"Wow! My baby got her first speaking engagement so quickly. I couldn't be a prouder father! I actually never thought I would see the day that you would become a professional speaker."

"You're not alone with that one," Nia replied, laughing in amazement. "My mind was so negative before, and I'm shocked that I would say 'not' after 'I can' when talking about anything I wanted to achieve."

"Growth mindset is so powerful. The Power of Yet is so powerful. I mean, the mind...is just so powerful. It can literally destroy you or manifest your thoughts into reality. It can grow you to heights you never could imagine you could see from a distance." Tears began streaming down her father's eyes as he clutched Nia tightly, his tears spilling on her yellow sweater. "I had to be honest with you and told you I wanted a son, but man, I'm so proud I had you Nia." Nia began growing emotional and shaking as she felt the warmth of her father's love. "So many black boys are losing their lives so early due to many things out of their control and within their control and it makes me grip you harder."

Nia shed abundant tears. The tears didn't seem to stop, like an everlasting stream of a waterfall. Tears of doubt were running away. Tears of a fixed mindset were leaving. Tears of contentment and satisfaction of fostering a growth mindset were planted. Tears of understanding The Power of Yet blossomed into the atmosphere. Tears of the mind's manifestation coming to fruition were expressed. All was well.

"I'm so proud you're my father as well, Dad."

As their tearful storms simmered, they glanced at one another and laughed, observing the red puffy glare in one another's eyes.

"Nia. Who are you and who am I?" He asked with a sniff.

"I'm Nia Akintewe, and you're my father who loves me!" She replied with a similar sniff.

"What do you deserve?"

"I deserve all the love in the world!"

"What are the three pillars for financial freedom to get rid of your student loan debt or overcome anything you encounter?"

"Believe. Plan. Execute."

"Why should you practice patience?"

"Patience allows me to take risks without repercussions, because it gives me the mindset to focus on the fact I have time."

"And why is gratitude so important?"

"You can't be great without being grateful, it's in the word if you reverse the letters."

"Amazing!"

"Dad!" Nia exclaimed happily. "I know the most important lesson I learned today and I'm ready to bless *you* with knowledge!"

"Shoot."

"I can't fear success, because it's a blessing in disguise!"

"Okay, that sounds spiritually powerful. I'm happy you understand that. Most people fear failure, so you're a bit of a contrarian with how you used to fear success, but I get you. The notion of people asking you for things because they feel entitled to your success is daunting. I can agree with that. And you never know who is friend or foe when you succeed. It always tends to be someone in your circle contributing something to a successful person's demise. Anything else you learned?"

"Thought you'd never ask!" Her smile widened. "I give up excuses with effort and discipline!"

"Now that sounds like a beautiful mentality to me. I see you've developed a strong mental acumen! Anything else ma'am?"

"The Compound Effect is Delayed Gratification! The Power of Yet means 'I Can!'"

"Wow! You sound like the gatekeeper of p-physicality. You've really grown to be an e-executor," he replied with a slight stammer.

Her father covered his face as if he had a migraine headache or sudden pain. Nia confusedly was taken aback.

"Dad! What happened?"

He revealed his face as he burst into tears once more, while Nia nearly imitated him.

"I was so lost at your age! I just wish when I was your age I knew all the information you possess now. It's just a beautiful thing to witness. I'm sure you'll understand one day."

"Thanks Dad. You know none of this would be possible without your guidance." She glanced up in the air as if she searched for tranquility from above, searching for The Power of Yet. "I'm reflecting, and I was misguided and very undecided; I failed so much I can't recollect how many times, but knowledge and wisdom were provided. Failure was that misguided and undecided Nia, while focus was the Nia that received that knowledge and wisdom. I'm grateful I can confidently say I focused more, and prevailed."

"Yes ma'am! Despite all the obstacles thrown at you, you prevailed. There was boredom, insecurities, fear, and more, but you maintained your spirit, mentality and physicality. All glory and honor be to God!"

"Failure was that misguided and undecided version of me I often saw in my dreams," Nia thought to herself, tuning out her father's words. "Focus was the Nia that listened to the knowledge and wisdom that was provided, eventually becoming so bright we couldn't stand near her in my dreams. It's crazy that was the difference for me between focus and failure. That's a simple mindset shift. That's a simple distinction between paying off my loans and taking decades to pay them off. But it's important to focus to fail to build character and vice versa to restore that motivation and drive to succeed. So did I not just focus but fail too? The mind is a scary concept."

"Whether or not you believe it, you've indirectly guided me as well. As a matter of fact, I have a new lesson I learned as well, Nia."

"What is it?"

"Reading books is such a special, powerful experience! I'm glad your primary intake of information isn't just those Facebook statuses and tweets you kids are always twittering. Reading is just so important. It's literally everywhere and improves your communication skills while allowing you the chance to practice applying information! Most importantly, it's a magical experience, because if you read any extensive piece of information, you're essentially downloading information that someone has spent a huge amount of time and thought into, instantly into your brain. That's a magical experience!"

"Okay? That's true, but I think I'm missing the point?"

"Listen, sweetie. Isn't that cool though? Someone spent hours, days, and even years of diligence and commitment to constructing a piece of work you can pick up and consume. It's like downloading it into your brain instantly and it becomes available to use like how a computer downloads files instantly and stores it. A book is the closest way to reach someone's mind, the author's thoughts painted on paper."

"Dad!"

"I've carefully recommended you several books I care about that helped shape who I am today, because I knew they would help shape who you became today as well."

"Dad! Can you get to the point for once?"

"Focus. I'm releasing my finished book, *The Power of Yet* during your first speaking engagement on Juneteenth. That'll be your next read."

PHYSICAL
EXERCISES

THE POWER OF EXECUTION!

In the physical phase, Nia learns the power of execution. She is a gatekeeper of the The Power of Yet and has the knowledge and wisdom for a growth mindset through her applied control of the spiritual, mental and physical phases. As we've reached the end of this experience, I encourage you to revisit the other phases for mastery and re-read the book in its entirety as needed. **The physical phase is controlled when you apply the power of execution.**

I want you to take out a piece of paper. You're going to write down something important that I want you to live and breathe each and every day. If you have student loan debt, this is for you. If you've paid off your loans already because this isn't your first time reading this book, customize your own question. The power of the written word is powerful, so write down your dreams into fruition!

Write down your student loan balance on a piece of paper. Write down a date you want to pay it off by. Fold this sheet of paper and carry it with you until you're debt free while reading it daily. Have a friend keep you accountable. Revisit this book's experience as needed for reiteration of any topics you require a motivational reset towards.

WHEN YOU <u>DO</u>, YOU'LL <u>SUCCEED</u>!

Nia learns the power of execution. We are going to practice execution. 99% of people think aimlessly, while 1% do. We are doers! Take out the sheet of paper you used to write your affirmation from the mental phase. Repeat your affirmation to yourself. Take out a separate piece of paper. Write down: fixed mindset.

Repeat this 3x: I (insert your name), rebuke the spirit of a fixed mindset in my life!

Ball the paper up and throw it in the trash can or light it on fire.

Now I am going to equip you with an additional affirmation to strengthen your growth mindset. Repeat after me:

I (insert your name), can't fear failure or success because it's a blessing in disguise! I (insert your name), give up excuses with effort and discipline! The Compound Effect is delayed gratification! The Power of Yet means I can and will have a growth mindset!

The physical phase is controlled when you apply the power of execution. *Take out a piece of paper and write this new affirmation down and keep it with you until you feel it breathing within your mind, body and soul effortlessly. Repeat this affirmation daily.*

THE POWER OF NOW!

Throughout Nia's journey, she was mentored by her father. Mentorship is important to personal development because when we are misguided and undecided, it's convenient to turn to someone that has experienced what we are currently experiencing. Now is the best time to be a mentor to someone!

No matter who you are reading this (yes you!), always remember that you're young (you're younger than your current age plus one) so now is the perfect time to start anything you aspire to achieve. Sometimes we simply need a reminder to keep moving forward, so I challenge you to be a mentee and go find someone to mentor you with your struggles!

Go find someone on the same path as you and walk together to conquer the journey. An additional mind is more potent than one. You've experienced traveling through three phases to help promote your growth mindset. Recommend this experience to a friend so the two of you may discuss its principles and reach the top of the mountain. I challenge both of you to perform your own 30 day challenge towards saving money that can be used for your student loans. Do it now!

The last exercise I have for you practices the importance of the power of this current beautiful moment we share together. Although this is the last exercise, the journey and your ascent is yet to be done.

The physical phase is controlled when you apply the power of execution.

Take out all the pieces of papers from each phase you've collected throughout this experience.

Re-read all your answers you've written down thus far. Do you still agree with all the ideas you wrote down? Do you still agree with your relationship with money? Meditate on your answers. Take one more look at all these answers before reading further.

You have the tools necessary to pay off your debt or accomplish anything you aim to achieve to a greater degree than you had prior to playing through this experience. You have the tools, but now you simply must execute in this current moment and apply everything you've learned along this journey.

This last exercise is a simple question:

Do you choose to focus or fail?

_____

_____

_____

_____

_____

_____

_____

_____

_____

_____

_____

_____

_____

ACKNOWLEDGMENTS

First and foremost, I want to thank God. All praise, honor and glory be to Him.

This book also wouldn't have been possible without the countless amazing human beings that helped facilitate my mind's ideas to translate from canvas to paper. Whether you're a close companion I communicate with daily or a couple times a year, I want to recognize you for your contribution to this experience you hold, or read on a screen. As I type this, I've just finished writing the final version of *The Power of Yet* and I'm on my couch listening to Chance The Rapper's "Everything's Good." I feel like that's the perfect way to describe this beautiful moment. No matter what our relationship is in the future, may peace and blessings be upon you.

I want to recognize those that have provided me with unconditional love and support along the way. It is with gratitude that I recognize the following amazing people:

Mom and Dad, thanks for all the unconditional love and support of anything I said I would do, no matter how outlandish it sounded.

Tope and Ayo, my older and younger brothers respectively, thanks for the support. Baby G's (Ayo) about to make another banger song! If you could relate, you could relate.

My couch and bed, thank y'all for supporting me as I've used y'all to complete most of this process.

I want to recognize those that have been there for me since day one and those that stepped into my life recently, allowing me to grow to enormous heights beyond my foresight. I want to recognize those that grind daily and motivate me to do the same. I want to recognize those that I've crossed paths with in my journey while immersing in Houston culture. I want to recognize those that have invested in my vision and challenged my ideas for my growth. I want to thank those that have inspired my financial journey towards financial freedom. I want to recognize those that have prayed for me. I want to recognize those that have helped me exercise my talents to start my speaking career. I want to recognize those that have supported me via social media and inspire me with their content. I want to thank those that trusted in my vision and gave me a platform to speak on topics as a mentor. I want to thank those that experienced unexpected situations with me, and I want to thank a person that inspired the creative philosophy behind this timeless piece. I want to thank those that mentored me when I was in Nia's position. It is with gratitude that I recognize the following amazing people:

Ja'Monie Ellis, Koyejo Ojuri, Nicholas Brown, Isaac Francis, Segunfunmitan Bamidele, Eric Thomas (ET), Gary Vaynerchuk, Ebun Akintewe, Gbogo Adebayo-Ige, Promise Adebayo-Ige, Dave Ramsey, John Lieu, Eden Aklile, Yashira Baggett, Skylar Greene, Matt Kucirek, Blessing Adogame, Ledornubari Nwilene, Ruben Cortez, Carol S. Dweck, Joseph Meacham, Jolyne Scholkowfsky and you, the reader.

I want to recognize a great person that contributed to my drive and hustle for this experience. It is with gratitude that I recognize the following amazing person:

Nipsey Hussle. R.I.P.

The marathon continues.

I want to recognize my writing team, because this journey wasn't possible without all of y'all adding pieces to the puzzle I couldn't complete myself. The hours of time and grind we put in day in and day out was worth this beautiful result. You all were patient with me in this process, because you knew I sincerely cared about this project and I appreciate y'all. I want to thank my book cover designer, my editors, my interior designer, my trailer creator, etc. It is with gratitude that I recognize the following amazing people:

Vlad Nicolaescu (much love to Romania), Nasima Sarder (much love to Bangladesh), Vincent Vi (much love to Vietnam) and my book editor, Blissblaze (much love to my land, Nigeria). Her edits are amazing! I recommend. You can find her on Fiverr at https://www.fiverr.com/blissblaze.

I want to recognize the National Society of Black Engineers (NSBE), an organization that's given me a number of life changing opportunities. I want to also recognize the NSBE chapters and the accompanying members I've governed that trusted my vision and allowed me to lead them. I want to also recognize the members around the world I've networked with.

I want to recognize those that have shown me mentorship when I was misguided and undecided, including my Thrive Mastermind group. We've been grinding day in and day out and it's crazy witnessing all the growth we've experienced over the past year. I know wherever y'all at, y'all can relate! It is with gratitude that I recognize the following amazing people:

Greg E. Hill, Jessica Bassett, Danny Blue, Doug Watson, and Lola Bradshaw.

I want to first recognize the music artists from Houston that have blessed millions around the world, including myself, with their brilliant talent and infectious culture. I also want to recognize the artists outside of Houston. As a whole, I want to recognize those music artists that have blessed the world with their wonderful vibrations. It is with gratitude that I recognize the following amazing people:

Beyoncé, Solange, DJ Screw, Megan Thee Stallion, Kendrick Lamar, Isaiah Rashad, Travis Scott, Tobe Nwigwe, Lecrae, Geto Boys, Scarface, Chamillionaire, Young Thug, Lil Baby, Gunna, C.J. Luckey, and Chance The Rapper.

I want to recognize the authors that have inspired me. It is with gratitude that I recognize the following amazing people:

Tomi Adeyemi, Angie Thomas, Don Miguel Ruiz, Tom Pace, Napoleon Hill, Paulo Coelho, Jeff Olson, and Darren Hardy.

I want to recognize the speakers and co-authors of a book that has inspired and influenced the direction of my speaking career. It is with gratitude that I recognize the following amazing people:

Linnita Hosten, Brian J. Olds, Les Brown, Dr. George C. Fraser, Dupé Aleru, Summer Alexander, Crystal Berger, Tiffany Bethea, Apryl Beverly, Horace Buddoo, Quinn Conyers, Marshall Fox, Reginal & Hennither Gant, Tierany Griffin, Mwalé & Chantel Henry, Kiaundra Jackson, Mothyna James-Brightful, Krista Jennings, Roquita Johnson, Dr. Will Moreland, Candice Nicole, Altovise Pelzer, Pam Perry, Keisha Reynolds, Shan-Nel Simmons, Kanika Tolver, Cliff Townsend, Danielle Tucker, Layna Ware, DeKesha Williams, LaKesha Womack, Cheryl Wood, and Robert T. "YB" Youngblood.

Speaking of authors, of course I have to thank myself. It is with gratitude that I recognize the following amazing person that took control of the spiritual, mental and physical battles tossed his way:

Michael Benjamin.

If I left your name out, don't take it personally. Get in contact with me and we can have a discussion of what happened.

I hope you enjoy *The Power of Yet* whether it be your first read or an additional read to reignite the flame you need to succeed.

—M.O.B., 2019

ABOUT THE AUTHOR

Michael Benjamin is an author, chemical engineer, financial coach and motivational speaker that speaks about mindfulness and its relation to overcoming various battles throughout the world. He enjoys following God to maximize his spiritual strength, exercising consistently to maintain his physical frame and implementing daily meditation and reading in his routine to maintain his mental acumen. He paid off $30,000+ in student loans in one year post-graduation at 23 years old and provides financial coaching services to others on how to do the same. You can follow Michael on Twitter and Instagram @ michobenjamin on both platforms and connect with him on LinkedIn. For more information, check out his website at:

www.michaelobenjamin.com

951-893-8081

59342488R00145

Made in the USA
Columbia, SC
04 June 2019